AF507277

Bible Devotions for Boys

Start Every Day Strong with Quick Devotions That Build Faith, Confidence, and a Brave Heart

Welcome Aboard, Check Out This Limited-Time Free Bonus!

Ahoy, reader! Welcome to the Ahoy Publications family, and thanks for snagging a copy of this book! Since you've chosen to join us on this journey, we'd like to offer you something special.

Check out the link below for a FREE e-book filled with delightful facts about American History.

But that's not all - you'll also have access to our exclusive email list with even more free e-books and insider knowledge. Well, what are ye waiting for? Click the link below to join and set sail toward exciting adventures in American History.

Access your bonus here
https://ahoypublications.com/
Or, Scan the QR code!

Table of Contents

Introduction
Start Every Day Strong

Some mornings feel easy. You wake up. You get dressed. You eat. You go.

Other mornings feel heavy. Your body is awake, but your heart feels tired. You might feel worried. You might feel mad. You might feel like you have to prove yourself.

God cares about all of that.

This book is for boys who want to walk with God in real life. At school. At home. On the field. Online. With friends. With family. When you win. When you mess up.

God does not ask you to be fake brave. He builds real strength in you. He grows faith in you. He teaches you how to stand firm and stay kind.

That is what a brave heart looks like.

<u>A PRAYER TO BEGIN</u>

God, Thank You for loving me. Thank You for giving me Your Word. Please help me listen and obey. Make my faith stronger. Build quiet courage in me. Help me be honest, kind, and brave. In Jesus' name, amen.

WEEK 1: Strong on the Inside

*"Have I not commanded you? Be strong and courageous.
Do not be afraid; do not be discouraged, for the Lord
your God will be with you wherever you go." -
Joshua 1:9*

Ethan stood by the door with his backpack on. It was the first day back at school.

His stomach felt tight. He kept thinking, *What if I mess up? What if kids laugh?* He tried to act tough, but his face still looked worried.

He opened his Bible and read today's verse out loud.

Ethan took a slow breath. He was still nervous, but he was not alone. He whispered, "God, help me today," and walked out the door.

<u>WHAT IT MEANS</u>

God spoke these words to Joshua before Joshua led God's people into a new land. Joshua had a big job. He needed courage.

This verse does not say, "Be brave because you are strong." It says, "Be brave because God is with you."

That changes everything.

You can feel scared and still do what is right. Courage is not the same as never feeling fear. Courage is obeying God even when your hands feel shaky.

God is with you at school, at practice, at home, and with your friends. He is with you in the hallway, at your desk, and at lunch. You do not have to pretend you are fine. You can ask God for help.

STRONG STEP

This week, choose **one** moment that feels hard.

- ✝ Raising your hand.
- ✝ Telling the truth.
- ✝ Saying sorry.
- ✝ Saying "no" to a bad idea.
- ✝ Sitting with someone who is alone.

Right before that moment, whisper: **"God is with me."**

Then, do the right thing. If you want, write "Joshua 1:9" on a small piece of paper and keep it in your pocket.

PRAYER

God, Please make me strong on the inside. Help me do what is right even when I feel scared. Thank You for being with me wherever I go. In Jesus' name, amen.

REMEMBER LINE

God is with me, so I can be brave.

WEEK 2: God Leads Me

"The Lord is my shepherd, I lack nothing." —
Psalm 23:1

Micah loved exploring. Behind his house was a patch of woods with a narrow trail. He had walked it many times, so he felt sure of himself.

One afternoon, he went a little farther than usual. He chased a lizard, climbed over a fallen log, and kept going. Soon the trail looked different. The trees felt closer together. The sun dropped lower.

Micah stopped. He turned around. Nothing looked familiar.

His heart started to beat fast. He did not want to call for help. He did not want anyone to know he had gotten turned around.

Then he remembered something his grandpa told him: "When you're lost, stop moving. Think. Ask for help."

Micah sat on a rock and took a slow breath. He whispered, "God, please lead me."

He listened. He heard a distant sound he knew: a dog barking near his neighbor's yard. Micah stood up and walked toward the sound. After a few minutes, he saw the edge of the woods. He was not far from home at all.

That night, Micah read Psalm 23. The first line stuck in his mind: "The LORD is my shepherd; I lack nothing."

<u>**WHAT IT MEANS**</u>

A shepherd leads sheep. Sheep are not good at finding safe paths. They get distracted. They wander. They need someone to guide them and keep them close.

God calls Himself a Shepherd because He cares for His people. He does not shout, "Figure it out!" He leads. He protects. He provides.

When the Bible says, "I lack nothing," it does not mean you get every toy or every win. It means this: with God as your Shepherd, you have what you truly need. You will not be left without His care. You can trust His path, even when you do not see the whole map.

This matters for real life. You will face choices. Some choices look fun but lead to trouble. Some choices feel hard but lead to peace.

A strong boy learns to say, "God, lead me," before he acts.

<u>**STRONG STEP**</u>

This week, practice the **Shepherd Check** before one decision each day.

1. **Stop:** Pause for ten seconds.
2. **Pray:** "Lord, please lead me."
3. **Choose:** Pick the path that fits God's Word: honest, kind, and wise.

Try it with choices like these:

† What to watch.

† What to say in a group chat.

† How to treat a kid who gets picked on.

† Whether to hide a mistake or tell the truth.

If you mess up, do not quit. Tell God the truth, ask forgiveness, and start again.

<u>**PRAYER**</u>

Lord, Thank You for being my Shepherd. Please lead me today. Help me want what is right, not what is wrong. Help me trust You when I feel unsure. In Jesus' name, amen.

<u>**REMEMBER LINE**</u>

God leads me, so I can choose the right path.

WEEK 3: Brave at Your Age

"Don't let anyone look down on you because you are young, but set an example for the believers in speech, in conduct, in love, in faith and in purity." -
1 Timothy 4:12

Jayden sat at the kitchen table, listening. His older sister and her friend were talking about a school project. They sounded stressed.

"We need someone to help with the poster," the friend said. "But it has to look good."

Jayden liked drawing. He had been practicing for months. He wanted to help, but he stayed quiet. He thought, *They won't take me seriously. I'm just a kid.*

Then his mom walked in and said, "Jayden, you're good at art. Want to help?"

Jayden's face got hot. Part of him wanted to say no and escape to his room. But he said, "I can try."

He worked carefully. He made the title bold. He drew clean lines. He added simple pictures that matched the topic. When he finished, he slid the poster across the table.

His sister stared for a second. "Wait ... you did this?"

Jayden nodded.

"It's actually amazing," she said, and she meant it.

Later that night, Jayden read a verse he had heard before: "Don't let anyone look down on you because you are young, but set an example for the believers in speech, in conduct, in love, in faith and in purity."

WHAT IT MEANS

Paul wrote these words to Timothy, who was a young leader in the church. Some people might have looked down on him because he was young. But Paul did not tell Timothy to whine or fight.

Paul told Timothy to live in a way that earned respect.

The rest of the verse explains how: be an example in speech, conduct, love, faith, and purity. That means your age does not stop God from using you. What matters is your character.

You can be brave at your age by doing things like these:

✝ Telling the truth when lying would be easier;

✝ Being kind when others are rude;

✝ Walking away from bad jokes;

✝ Working hard when nobody is clapping; and

✝ Honoring God when friends do not.

A brave heart does not say, "I'm too young to matter." A brave heart says, "God can help me live right today."

STRONG STEP

This week, pick **one area** to be an example.

Choose one: **words, actions, love, faith, or purity.**

Then do one clear thing:

✝ **Words:** Speak without insults for one whole day.

✝ **Actions:** Do one chore without being asked.

✝ **Love:** Include someone who is left out.

✝ **Faith:** Pray for one minute before school.

✝ **Purity:** Turn away from something you know is wrong, right away.

Tell God what you picked. Ask for help. Then do it again the next day.

<u>**PRAYER**</u>

God, Thank You that You can use me right now. Help me be an example, even though I'm young. Give me brave strength to do what is right. In Jesus' name, amen.

<u>**REMEMBER LINE**</u>

I can honor God, even at my age.

WEEK 4: Real Love in Real Life

"Love is patient, love is kind. It does not envy, it does not boast, it is not proud." - 1 Corinthians 13:4

Noah's little brother, Miles, followed him everywhere.

When Noah built a LEGO set, Miles wanted to help. When Noah played a game, Miles wanted a turn. When Noah tried to read, Miles asked questions. A lot of questions.

One Saturday, Noah finally snapped. "Go away, Miles! You ruin everything!"

Miles froze. His eyes got watery. He walked to his room without a word.

Noah felt a hot sting in his chest. He did not like what he had done, but he also did not want to admit it. He tried to play again, but the game was not fun anymore.

Later, Noah saw Miles sitting on the floor with a broken toy. Miles was trying to fix it with his small hands. Noah could have ignored him. Instead, he sat down.

"Hey," Noah said quietly. "I was mean. I'm sorry."

Miles looked up. "You don't like me?"

Noah swallowed hard. "I do. I just got annoyed. I want to do better."

Noah helped fix the toy. Then he let Miles pick the next game.

That night, Noah read this line: "Love is patient, love is kind." It felt simple, but it hit him right where he needed it.

WHAT IT MEANS

Love is more than a feeling. In the Bible, love is a way you treat people.

Patience means you do not explode fast. Kindness means you use your strength to help, not hurt.

This verse does not say, "Love is easy." It says love is patient and kind, especially when you feel annoyed.

Real love shows up in normal moments:

✟ When your brother wants to tag along.

✟ When your mom asks you to do something again.

✟ When a friend is slow to understand.

✟ When someone makes a mistake.

A brave heart does not use anger to control people. A brave heart chooses patience and kindness because Jesus loves you that way.

STRONG STEP

Try the **Pause and Kindness Plan** one time each day this week.

1. **Pause:** Stop for three seconds before you speak.
2. **Pick kind words:** Say what is true without being harsh.
3. **Do one kind action:** Help, share, or encourage.

Here are a few kind actions:

✟ Carry something heavy for someone.

✟ Let a younger kid go first.

✟ Send a short message that builds someone up.

✟ Say, "I'm sorry," fast instead of slow.

PRAYER

God, Thank You for loving me with patience and kindness. Please help me love like that today. Help me slow down when I feel annoyed. Make my words and actions kind. In Jesus' name, amen.

REMEMBER LINE

Love looks like patience and kindness.

WEEK 5: Truth-Talker

"Therefore each of you must put off falsehood and speak truthfully to your neighbor, for we are all members of one body." - Ephesians 4:25

Caleb was rushing to finish his homework when his elbow bumped his cup. Water splashed across the table and soaked his sister's library book.

Caleb froze. The cover started to curl.

He grabbed a towel and wiped fast, but the pages still looked wavy. His heart pounded. He thought, *If I tell the truth, I'll get in trouble. If I hide it, maybe no one will notice.*

His sister walked in. "Have you seen my book?"

Caleb held it behind his back. "Uh ... no."

The lie came out quick. Too quick.

His sister searched around, getting more upset. Caleb felt worse with every second. His stomach hurt, and his face felt hot. The lie did not protect him. It trapped him.

Caleb finally pulled the book out. "I spilled water on it. I'm sorry. I got scared."

His sister stared at the book, then at Caleb. "Why didn't you just tell me?"

"I didn't want you to be mad," Caleb said.

She sighed. "I am mad. But I'd rather you tell the truth."

That night, Caleb read: "Speak the truth." It felt like God was talking straight to him.

WHAT IT MEANS

Lying seems like a quick escape, but it always costs something. It breaks trust. It makes your heart feel heavy. It can also hurt other people.

God tells His people to put away falsehood. That means we do not keep lies like tools in our pocket. We do not save them "just in case."

The verse also says to speak truth "with his neighbor." That includes family, friends, teammates, classmates, and teachers. Truth is part of love because it treats people with respect.

Telling the truth takes courage. It might mean you face a consequence. But truth keeps your heart clean and your relationships strong.

A brave heart is honest, even when it is hard.

STRONG STEP

Practice the **Truth Habit** this week.

When you mess up, do these three things:

1. **Say it fast:** Tell the truth as soon as you can.
2. **Say it clear:** No excuses, no blaming.
3. **Make it right:** Ask, "What can I do to fix this?"

Here are examples you can use:

† "I broke it. I'm sorry."

† "That was my fault."

† "I lied, and I want to tell the truth now."

The first time feels tough. The next time gets easier.

PRAYER

God, Please make me an honest boy. Help me tell the truth even when I'm afraid. Forgive me when I lie. Teach me to make things right. In Jesus' name, amen.

REMEMBER LINE

Truth takes courage, and God helps me be honest.

WEEK 6: Calm Words, Strong Boy

Liam was building a model plane at the kitchen table. He had been saving his money for it, and he wanted it to look perfect.

His cousin, Ben, came over and leaned in close. "Let me see!"

Before Liam could answer, Ben's hand bumped the wing. *Snap.* A small piece broke off and slid across the table.

Liam's face got hot. "What is wrong with you?" he yelled. "You always ruin stuff!"

Ben's eyes went wide. He stepped back like he had been pushed. "I didn't mean to."

Liam grabbed the broken piece. His hands were shaking. He wanted to say more. He wanted Ben to feel bad.

Then Liam remembered a verse he had heard in Sunday school: "A gentle answer turns away wrath."

Liam swallowed. He took one slow breath. "Ben," he said, still upset, "I'm really mad because I worked hard on this."

Ben nodded fast. "I'm sorry. I'll help fix it."

Liam pointed to the glue. "Okay. Just ... be careful."

The room felt calmer. The problem was still real, but now it was getting solved instead of getting worse.

WHAT IT MEANS

Words can be like fuel on a fire. A harsh word can turn a small mistake into a big fight. A gentle answer can stop the fire before it spreads.

Gentle does not mean weak. Gentle means controlled. It means you choose your words instead of letting anger choose for you.

This verse shows two paths:

✝ **Harsh words** stir up anger. They add heat, blame, and pain.

✝ **Gentle answers** turn away wrath. They lower the temperature and make space to fix the problem.

A brave heart is strong enough to stay steady. That is real strength.

You can still be honest about what happened. You can still say, "That hurt," or "That was wrong." But you can say it in a way that helps instead of harms.

STRONG STEP

Try the **Soft Start** this week when you feel anger rising.

1. **Pause:** Stop and breathe once.
2. **Name it:** Say what you feel without insults.
3. **Aim for peace:** Ask for a good next step.

Here are gentle starters you can use:

✝ "I'm upset. Please stop."

✝ "That wasn't okay. Let's fix it."

✝ "I need a minute to calm down."

If you blow up, do not stay stuck. Go back and repair it: "I was harsh. I'm sorry. Let me try again."

PRAYER

God, Please help me control my words. When I feel angry, help me pause and speak gently. Make me strong enough to bring peace. In Jesus' name, amen.

REMEMBER LINE

Gentle words can stop a fight.

WEEK 7: Trust First

"Trust in the Lord with all your heart and lean not on your own understanding;" - Proverbs 3:5

Aiden's coach called him over after practice. "Try out for the next level team," the coach said. "You're ready."

Aiden nodded, but his chest felt tight.

That night he lay in bed thinking about everything that could go wrong. What if I mess up? What if I get cut? What if everyone is better than me?

The tryout was on Saturday. All week, Aiden's worry kept tapping him on the shoulder.

On Friday, his dad found him sitting quiet on the couch. "You okay?"

Aiden shrugged. "I don't know if I should even go."

His dad did not laugh. He said, "It's normal to feel nervous. But you don't have to let fear drive."

Aiden opened his Bible and read one line: "Trust in the LORD with all your heart."

He thought about that word **all**. Not half. Not only when he felt confident. All.

Aiden whispered, "God, I trust You with Saturday." Then he got up and packed his bag.

<u>**WHAT IT MEANS**</u>

Trust means you place weight on something. Like sitting in a chair. You sit because you believe it will hold you.

When the Bible says, "Trust in the LORD," it means God can hold your life. He can hold your future. He can hold your fear.

Trust is not pretending everything will be easy. Trust is saying, "God is good, even if I don't know what will happen next."

Sometimes God changes your situation. Sometimes He changes your heart while you walk through it. Either way, He is faithful.

A brave heart learns to trust God first, before worry grows big.

<u>**STRONG STEP**</u>

Do the **Trust Swap** once each day this week.

1. Name one worry out loud. Keep it short.
   - "I'm worried about the test."
   - "I'm worried about my friends."
2. Pray one simple sentence:
   - "God, I trust You with this."
3. Take one wise step you can control.
   - Study ten minutes.
   - Apologize.
   - Ask for help.
   - Do your job at home.

Trust is not sitting still. Trust is doing the right next thing with God.

<u>**PRAYER**</u>

God, You know what I'm worried about. Help me trust You with all my heart. Please lead me and give me peace. In Jesus' name, amen.

<u>**REMEMBER LINE**</u>

I trust God first, even when I feel nervous.

WEEK 8: Not Alone

"So do not fear, for I am with you; do not be dismayed, for I am your God. I will strengthen you and help you; I will uphold you with my righteous right hand." - Isaiah 41:10

Connor stood at the edge of the lunch area with his tray. The room felt loud. Kids were talking fast, laughing, trading snacks.

Connor scanned the tables. His best friend was absent. The seat Connor usually sat in was taken.

He walked to one table, then stopped. Nobody looked up. He felt like his feet were glued to the floor.

Connor wanted to turn around and eat in the bathroom. He had heard kids do that. He hated that idea, but he also hated feeling invisible.

His hand shook a little as he held the tray. He whispered, so quiet nobody could hear, "God, please be with me."

A Bible phrase popped into his mind from church: "Fear not, for I am with you."

Connor took one slow breath and walked to a table with one open spot. He pointed to the chair and asked, "Can I sit here?"

A boy shrugged. "Sure."

Connor sat down. He ate. He did not talk much at first. But he stayed. And that was brave.

WHAT IT MEANS

Fear can show up in normal places. It can show up in a noisy hallway. It can show up when you feel left out. It can show up when you think everyone is watching you.

God does not ignore fear. He speaks to it.

"Fear not" is not a rude command, like, "Stop it." It is a loving reminder: "I am with you."

God is with you when you feel alone. He is with you when friends are not around. He is with you when you have to take the first step.

Sometimes God helps by changing what happens around you. Sometimes He helps by giving you steady courage inside. Either way, His presence is real.

A brave heart remembers this: being alone in a room is not the same as being alone in life. God is there.

STRONG STEP

Try the **With-Me Move** this week.

When you feel fear, do these three things:

1. **Say the phrase:** "God is with me."
2. **Take one small step:** walk up, speak up, or stay calm.
3. **Thank God after:** "Thank You for helping me."

Small steps count. A "hello" counts. Sitting down counts. Asking for help counts.

PRAYER

God, Sometimes I feel alone or nervous. Thank You that You are with me. Please help me take the brave next step today. In Jesus' name, amen.

REMEMBER LINE

I'm not alone. God is with me.

WEEK 9: Pure Heart, Pure Choices

*"Create in me a pure heart, O God, and renew a
steadfast spirit within me." - Psalm 51:10*

Owen was watching videos on a tablet when a clip popped up that didn't feel right. It wasn't the kind of thing he would want his mom to see. It also left a gross feeling in his stomach.

He told himself, *Just scroll. No big deal.* But his thumb stopped. Part of him wanted to keep looking. Another part of him wanted to shut it down fast.

Owen turned the screen off and set the tablet on the couch. His heart was beating harder than it should have.

He walked to his room and sat on his bed. He felt confused and a little ashamed. He didn't know what to do with that feeling.

So he did something honest. He prayed, "God, my heart feels messy. Please help me."

Then he opened his Bible to the Psalms and read today's verse.

Owen did not feel perfect in one second, but he felt relief. God could clean what felt dirty inside.

WHAT IT MEANS

King David prayed this verse after he sinned. He did not excuse it. He did not blame others. He went to God and asked for a clean heart.

A pure heart does not mean you never see something wrong or never get tempted. It means you do not keep sin close. You bring your heart to God and ask Him to make it right.

Your heart is like the control center of your life. What you watch, what you think about, and what you laugh at can shape your choices. That is why God cares about your heart.

God is not scared of your struggle. He wants you to come to Him quickly. When you confess your sin, He listens. He forgives. He helps you choose better next time.

A brave heart is not a boy who never gets tempted. A brave heart is a boy who runs to God when he is tempted.

STRONG STEP

Do the **Clean Switch** this week.

When you see or hear something you know is wrong:

1. **Switch it off fast:** close it, scroll away, walk out.
2. **Tell God right away:** "God, clean my heart."
3. **Fill your mind with good:** read a Bible verse, do something active, or talk to someone you trust.

If you need help, tell a parent or caregiver. That is not weakness. That is wisdom.

PRAYER

God, Please create in me a clean heart. Help me turn away from what is wrong. Forgive me when I mess up. Teach me to love what is good. In Jesus' name, amen.

REMEMBER LINE

God can clean my heart, and He can help me choose right.

WEEK 10: Do It for God

"So whether you eat or drink or whatever you do, do it all for the glory of God." - 1 Corinthians 10:31

Tyler was taking out the trash when he saw the bag had a leak. Old juice dripped onto the floor.

Tyler groaned. *Not my problem,* he thought. He could toss the bag outside and pretend he didn't notice. His mom might think the dog did it. Or his little sister.

He stepped toward the door ... then stopped.

Tyler remembered something his youth leader said: "God sees the stuff nobody claps for."

Tyler grabbed paper towels and cleaned the floor. Then he took the trash out and tied a new bag in the can.

When he finished, nobody cheered. Nobody even noticed.

Tyler smiled anyway. He whispered, "God, I did that for You."

<u>WHAT IT MEANS</u>

This verse shows that God cares about your whole life, not just church days. "Whatever you do" includes homework, chores, sports, and how you treat people when you're tired.

Doing something "to the glory of God" means you do it in a way that honors Him. You do it with honesty. You do it with effort. You do it with a good attitude, even when nobody is watching.

That kind of faith builds strong confidence. Why? Because you are not living for likes or applause. You are living to please God.

A brave heart works hard even in small things.

STRONG STEP

Try the **God-First Finish** this week.

Pick one small job you usually rush or complain about:

† Making your bed.

† Loading the dishwasher.

† Feeding a pet.

† Finishing homework.

† Putting your shoes away.

Do it all the way through. No shortcuts. No grumbling.

Then say one sentence to God: **"I did this for You."**

PRAYER

God, Help me honor You in what I do today. Help me work hard and stay honest. Teach me to do small things with a strong heart. In Jesus' name, amen.

REMEMBER LINE

I can honor God in everyday stuff.

WEEK 11: Ask God for Help

"Ask and it will be given to you; seek and you will find; knock and the door will be opened to you." - Matthew 7:7

Dylan stared at the math page. The numbers looked like they were dancing.

He tried the first problem. Wrong. He tried the second. Wrong again.

Dylan's face got hot. He wanted to crumple the paper and say, "I'm just bad at this." He also didn't want to ask for help. What if his teacher sighed? What if his dad got annoyed?

Dylan pushed his chair back and walked to the sink for a drink. He looked out the window and whispered, "God, help me understand."

Then he went back to the table and did something else brave. He asked his mom, "Can you show me the first step?"

His mom sat down. "Sure. Let's do one together."

They worked slowly. Dylan noticed a pattern. The page still wasn't easy, but now it made sense.

Later, Dylan read Jesus' words: "Ask ... seek ... knock." It felt like a clear plan for boys who don't have all the answers.

<u>**WHAT IT MEANS**</u>

Jesus tells you to ask because God is not annoyed by your needs. He is a good Father.

"Ask" means you pray and tell God what you need. "Seek" means you keep looking for the right way, not the lazy way. "Knock" means you don't quit after one try.

This verse is not a promise that you get anything you want, like a vending machine. It is a promise that God listens and responds in the right way and the right time.

God often helps in more than one way. Sometimes, He gives peace. Sometimes, He gives wisdom. Sometimes, He sends a person to help you, but it starts with asking.

A brave heart is humble enough to say, "I need help."

<u>**STRONG STEP**</u>

Use the **Ask-Seek-Knock Plan** once a day this week.

1. **Ask God:** "Please help me with ____."
2. **Seek:** Do one smart step you can do.
3. **Knock:** If you're still stuck, ask a person for help.

People you can "knock" on: a parent, a teacher, a coach, or a trusted adult at church.

Try it with schoolwork, friendships, temptation, or fear.

<u>**PRAYER**</u>

God, Thank You that You hear me. Please help me with what I'm facing today. Give me wisdom and courage to keep trying. In Jesus' name, amen.

<u>**REMEMBER LINE**</u>

I can ask God for help, and I can keep trying.

WEEK 12: Big Forgiveness

"Jesus answered, "I tell you, not seven times, but seventy-seven times.." - Matthew 18:22

Riley and his friend Mason had been building a fort behind the garage for three days. They used boards, old blankets, and a sign that said "NO GIRLS ALLOWED."

On the fourth day, Riley ran outside and stopped cold. Part of the fort had fallen down. A board was cracked.

Mason stood there, kicking the dirt. "I leaned on it," he said. "It broke."

Riley's hands clenched into fists. "Why would you do that?" he shouted. "You ruin everything!"

Mason's face fell. "I didn't mean to. I tried to fix it, but it got worse."

Riley wanted to say, "We're done. We're not friends." He wanted Mason to feel the pain too.

Then Riley remembered a lesson from church about forgiveness. He didn't like it, but he remembered it.

Riley took a breath. "I'm mad," he said, "but I don't want to hold this against you."

Mason looked up. "Really?"

Riley nodded. "Yeah. Let's fix it."

They grabbed tools and worked together. The fort didn't look perfect after, but the friendship felt stronger.

WHAT IT MEANS

Peter asked Jesus how many times he had to forgive someone. Peter thought he was being generous when he said "seven times."

Jesus answered with a number so big it meant this: keep forgiving.

Jesus was not saying you should let people hurt you over and over without help. If someone is unsafe or cruel, you must tell a trusted adult. Forgiveness is not the same as pretending wrong is okay.

Forgiveness means you choose not to hold the offense like a weapon. You let go of payback. You give the problem to God. You can still set wise boundaries, but you don't keep hate in your heart.

Forgiveness takes courage. It can feel like losing. But it is actually strong. It frees you from carrying heavy anger.

A brave heart forgives because Jesus forgives.

STRONG STEP

Try the **Forgive and Build** plan this week.

1. **Name it:** "That hurt me."
2. **Choose it:** "I forgive you."
3. **Build peace:** If it's safe, take one step to make it right.

Examples of "build peace":

- ✝ Talk it out calmly.
- ✝ Fix what got broken.
- ✝ Invite the person back in.
- ✝ Pray for help to let it go.

If you keep replaying it in your mind, tell God again: "I forgive. Help my heart catch up."

PRAYER

Jesus, Thank You for forgiving me. Help me forgive others when they hurt me. Take anger out of my heart and replace it with peace. Give me wisdom when I need help from an adult. In Your name, amen.

REMEMBER LINE

I forgive because Jesus forgave me.

WEEK 13: Listen First

"My dear brothers and sisters, take note of this: Everyone should be quick to listen, slow to speak and slow to become angry," - James 1:19

Marcus was sure he heard his name. He was walking past a group of boys when one of them laughed. Another one whispered something.

Marcus felt a spark of anger. *They're talking about me.*

He spun around. "What did you say?" he snapped.

The boys looked surprised. "Nothing," one said. "We were talking about a video."

Marcus didn't believe them. His voice got louder. "Yeah, right."

A teacher nearby glanced over. The group got quiet. Marcus felt his face burn. Now he looked like the problem.

Later, Marcus sat on his bed and replayed it. He wasn't even sure what they said. He just reacted.

That night he opened his Bible and read: "Quick to listen, slow to speak, and slow to become angry."

Marcus whispered, "I didn't do that."

<u>**WHAT IT MEANS**</u>

This verse is like a guardrail for your mouth and your temper.

"Quick to hear" means you listen before you decide what is true. "Slow to speak" means you don't fire words like arrows. "Slow to anger" means you don't let one moment control your whole day.

Listening first is not weakness. It is wisdom. It keeps you from jumping to the wrong conclusion. It also helps you treat people fairly.

A brave heart can pause. A brave heart can ask, "What's really going on?" before it reacts.

You can still stand up for yourself. You can still say, "That's not okay." But first, listen and make sure you understand.

<u>**STRONG STEP**</u>

Try the **Three-Second Rule** this week.

When you feel annoyed, do this:

1. **Pause for three seconds.**
2. **Ask one calm question:** "What do you mean?" or "Can you say that again?"
3. **Then answer** with steady words.

If you already snapped, go back and repair it: "I spoke too fast. I'm sorry. Tell me what happened."

<u>**PRAYER**</u>

God, Help me listen first. Slow down my mouth and my anger. Give me wisdom to understand before I react. In Jesus' name, amen.

<u>**REMEMBER LINE**</u>

I will listen first and speak last.

WEEK 14: Faith That Moves

Santi saw the new kid sitting alone at recess. The kid's name was Eli. He stayed near the fence and watched everyone else play.

Santi felt a nudge in his heart. *Go say hi.*

But another thought pushed back. *What if it's awkward? What if my friends think it's weird?*

Santi told himself, *I'll pray for him.* That sounded good. But Santi also knew something: he could pray and still walk over.

So Santi took a breath and headed toward the fence.

"Hey," he said. "I'm Santi. Want to play soccer with us?"

Eli looked surprised. Then he nodded. "Okay."

On the field, Eli didn't talk much at first. But after a few passes, he smiled. By the end of recess, he was running and calling for the ball like he belonged there.

That afternoon, Santi remembered a verse: "Faith by itself, if it is not accompanied by action, is dead." It made sense. Faith isn't just words. Faith moves your feet.

WHAT IT MEANS

Faith means you trust God, but real trust shows up in what you do.

If you say, "I believe God wants me to be kind," but you never act kindly, something is missing. The Bible calls that "dead" faith. Not because faith is useless, but because faith was meant to live and move.

Works do not save you. Jesus saves you, but faith that belongs to Jesus changes how you live.

A brave heart doesn't just think about doing good. It does good. It obeys God in small, real ways.

STRONG STEP

Do **One Faith Move** this week.

Pick one action that matches what you believe:

- ✝ Sit with someone who is alone.
- ✝ Share what you have.
- ✝ Tell the truth about a mistake.
- ✝ Pray for someone and then encourage them.
- ✝ Help at home without being asked.

Keep it simple. Do it on purpose. Then thank God for helping you act.

If you feel nervous, whisper: **"God, help my faith move."**

PRAYER

God, Thank You for saving me through Jesus. Help my faith be real, not just words. Show me one good thing to do this week, and help me do it. In Jesus' name, amen.

REMEMBER LINE

Real faith shows up in real actions.

WEEK 15: Ready for Battle

Kai had a good day at school. Then he got home and checked his phone.

One message popped up in the class chat: A joke about him. Then another. Then a laughing emoji. More boys piled on.

Kai's face went hot. He wanted to fire back. He wanted to type something that would sting. His thumbs hovered over the screen.

Then he remembered something his mom said: "Your biggest battles aren't always with fists. Sometimes they're with words."

Kai set the phone down and took a breath. He walked to his room and opened his Bible. His eyes landed on a short phrase: "Put on the whole armor of God."

Kai thought about armor. Armor doesn't make a soldier mean. Armor helps a soldier stand.

Kai picked up his phone again, but this time he chose a different move. He didn't join the trash talk. He muted the chat and told his mom what happened.

That night, he prayed for help to do the right thing tomorrow.

WHAT IT MEANS

God tells you to put on His armor because you have real battles. Some battles are outside you, like pressure from other kids. Some battles are inside you, like anger, jealousy, and temptation.

Armor is not for showing off. Armor is for protection.

God's armor helps you stand firm when lies hit your mind, when people push you to sin, or when you feel alone. It helps you choose what is right even when wrong feels easier.

You don't put on armor with your hands. You put it on with your choices:

- ✝ You choose truth instead of lies.
- ✝ You choose right actions instead of wrong actions.
- ✝ You choose peace instead of revenge.
- ✝ You choose God's Word instead of empty noise.

A brave heart prepares before the fight shows up.

STRONG STEP

Try the **Armor Check** each morning this week. It takes one minute.

- ✝ **Truth:** "God, help me tell the truth today."
- ✝ **Right:** "Help me do what is right."
- ✝ **Peace:** "Help me stay calm and make peace."
- ✝ **Faith:** "Help me trust You."
- ✝ **God's Word:** "Help me remember one Bible phrase."

Then pick **one** place you need armor most: school, sports, online, or home. Ask God to guard you there.

PRAYER

God, Please help me put on Your armor today. Guard my mind and my words. Help me stand strong when I feel pressure to do wrong. In Jesus' name, amen.

REMEMBER LINE

God's armor helps me stand strong.

WEEK 16: Worry to Prayer

"Do not be anxious about anything, but in every situation, by prayer and petition, with thanksgiving, present your requests to God." - Philippians 4:6

Brandon's mom taped a note to the fridge: **Dentist. Tuesday. 3:30.**

Brandon stared at it every time he walked by. He hated the sound of the drill. He hated the bright light. He hated not knowing what they would say.

On Tuesday morning, his worry was already awake. His shoulders felt tight at breakfast. At school he couldn't focus. His brain kept replaying the same scary picture.

After school, Brandon sat in the car and tried to act normal. But his foot bounced fast.

His mom glanced over. "You're quiet."

Brandon finally said it. "I'm worried. What if it hurts?"

His mom nodded. "That's real. Let's pray."

Right there in the car, Brandon closed his eyes. "God, I'm scared," he whispered. "Please help me."

Then his mom added, "Thank You that Brandon is not alone. Please give him peace."

Brandon still didn't love the dentist. But his chest felt lighter. He wasn't carrying the worry by himself anymore.

<u>**WHAT IT MEANS**</u>

Worry shows up when you keep thinking, *What if something bad happens?* It can feel like a heavy backpack you can't take off.

This verse does not say, "Never feel nervous." It says, "Don't live in anxiety." There's a difference.

God gives you a better path: prayer.

"Prayer and supplication" means you talk to God about what you need. You can be honest. You can say, "I'm scared," or "I don't know what to do."

And then it says "with thanksgiving." That means you thank God for what is true right now:

✝ God hears you.

✝ God is with you.

✝ God has helped you before.

Prayer doesn't always remove the hard thing. But it puts God in the middle of it, and that changes your heart.

A brave heart doesn't hide worry. It hands worry to God.

<u>**STRONG STEP**</u>

Use the **Worry List** this week.

1. Write down **three** worries on a small paper.
2. Pray over each one, one sentence each.
3. After each worry, say one thank-you: "Thank You, God, that You are with me."

Example:

✝ "God, I'm worried about the test. Please help me study. Thank You for giving me a brain to learn."

Keep the paper in your room. If worry returns, pray again.

<u>**PRAYER**</u>

God, You know what I'm worried about. I bring it to You right now. Please help me and give me peace. Thank You for listening to me. In Jesus' name, amen.

<u>**REMEMBER LINE**</u>

When I worry, I pray and thank God.

WEEK 17: Strength for Hard Days

"I can do all this through him who gives me strength." -
Philippians 4:13

Nate's legs felt like jelly halfway through the mile run in P.E. His lungs burned. The other boys looked like they were flying past him.

Nate slowed down. A thought hit him hard: *I'm the slow kid. Everyone knows it.*

He wanted to quit. He wanted to walk and pretend his shoe was tied.

Then he saw a smaller boy ahead of him. That boy was struggling too. Nate thought, *If he can keep going, I can keep going.*

Nate whispered, "God, give me strength." He didn't shout it. He just said it like a real request.

He kept moving. Not fast. But steady. Step after step.

When he crossed the line, he wasn't first. But he finished. And he didn't quit.

Later, Nate read: "I can do all things through him who strengthens me." He knew it didn't mean he could instantly become the best runner. It meant God could help him stay faithful in hard moments.

WHAT IT MEANS

This verse is often used like it means, "I can do anything I want." But Paul wrote it while facing very hard days. He learned to be content when life felt tough.

So what does it mean for you?

It means Jesus can strengthen you to do what is right. He can help you keep going when you want to stop. He can help you do hard things like:

✝ Finishing your work.

✝ Controlling your temper.

✝ Walking away from temptation.

✝ Telling the truth.

✝ Trying again after a failure.

God's strength often feels like steady help, not a sudden burst. He gives enough strength for the next step.

A brave heart doesn't depend on feelings. It depends on God.

STRONG STEP

This week, practice the **Next Step Prayer**.

When something feels hard, do this:

1. Whisper: **"Jesus, strengthen me."**
2. Ask: "What is my next right step?"
3. Do that one step.

Examples:

✝ If homework feels hard: do the first problem.

✝ If you're angry: take a walk and cool down.

✝ If you're tempted: turn away and tell an adult.

Small steps, done with God, build strong confidence.

PRAYER

Jesus, Please strengthen me today. Help me do the next right thing when life feels hard. Thank You that I don't have to quit. In Your name, amen.

REMEMBER LINE

Jesus gives me strength for the next step.

WEEK 18: Strong Enough to Serve

"You, my brothers and sisters, were called to be free. But do not use your freedom to indulge the flesh; rather, serve one another humbly in love." - Galatians 5:13

It was Saturday morning, and Eli wanted to play video games. He had been thinking about it all week.

Then his mom said, "Can you help me bring groceries in?"

Eli sighed. He didn't say no, but his face did. He walked to the car slow, like each step was heavy.

On the second trip, he saw his neighbor Mrs. Thompson struggling with a big bag of dog food. She was small, and the bag looked heavy.

Eli could have pretended he didn't notice, but he didn't.

"Do you want help?" he asked.

Mrs. Thompson looked relieved. "Yes, please."

Eli carried the bag to her porch. She smiled. "Thank you, young man."

Eli felt something warm in his chest. He hadn't gotten points or money. But he felt good, like he did something that mattered.

Later, Eli read: "Through love serve one another." He realized serving wasn't just chores. It was love in action.

<u>**WHAT IT MEANS**</u>

Serving means using your strength to help someone else. It can be big, like helping someone in a real crisis. It can also be small, like picking up a dropped pencil.

God doesn't want you to serve so people think you're a hero. He wants you to serve because love is real.

Sometimes pride says, "I'm too important." Sometimes laziness says, "Someone else will do it." But love says, "I can help."

Jesus served people all the time. He helped the weak. He cared for the overlooked. He washed feet. He gave His time. He gave His life.

When you serve, you become more like Jesus. That builds a brave heart.

<u>**STRONG STEP**</u>

Do **One Quiet Serve** this week. Quiet means you don't announce it. Pick one:

- ✝ Take out the trash without being asked.
- ✝ Help a sibling with a task.
- ✝ Hold the door for someone.
- ✝ Carry something heavy.
- ✝ Clean up a mess that isn't yours.

After you do it, say to God: **"I did that through love."**

<u>**PRAYER**</u>

God, Thank You for loving me. Help me serve others with a willing heart. Show me someone I can help this week. In Jesus' name, amen.

<u>**REMEMBER LINE**</u>

Love serves, even when it's not fun.

WEEK 19: Grow Good Fruit

"But the fruit of the Spirit is love, joy, peace, forbearance, kindness, goodness, faithfulness, gentleness and self-control. Against such things there is no law." -
Galatians 5:22–23

Logan had a plan. He was going to stay calm all day.

But by lunchtime, his plan was falling apart.

A kid cut in line. Someone bumped his shoulder. His friend teased him. Logan felt his patience leaking out like a balloon.

In the afternoon, Logan sat in class tapping his pencil hard. His teacher walked by and said softly, "Logan, take a breath."

Logan did. One breath. Then another.

After school, he walked home and saw his little sister trying to ride her bike. She kept wobbling and putting her foot down. "I can't do it!" she yelled.

Logan almost said, "I'm busy." But he stopped. He remembered a verse from church about "fruit."

He set down his bag. "I'll help," he said.

He ran beside her, holding the seat steady. "Keep pedaling. You've got it."

She tried again. This time she stayed up longer. She smiled wide. Logan smiled too.

Later, Logan read the list: love, joy, peace, patience, kindness, goodness, faithfulness, gentleness, self-control. He realized God was growing these things in him, one choice at a time.

WHAT IT MEANS

Fruit grows on a tree over time. It doesn't pop out in one second.

The "fruit of the Spirit" means these good qualities grow in you when God's Spirit is at work in you. You can't grow them by willpower alone. But you can choose to follow God instead of your anger, your laziness, or your pride.

This list is also a mirror. It helps you ask, "What am I growing?"

✝ When you choose kindness, kindness grows.

✝ When you practice self-control, self-control grows.

✝ When you forgive, peace grows.

A brave heart lets God shape it. It doesn't stay stuck.

STRONG STEP

Try the **Fruit Pick** this week.

1. Choose **one** fruit from the list that you need most. (patience, kindness, self-control, or another)

2. Each morning, pray: "God, grow ______ in me today."

3. Look for one moment to practice it.

Example:

✝ **Patience:** don't snap when you have to wait.

✝ **Kindness:** say one encouraging sentence.

✝ **Self-control:** stop yourself before a bad choice.

Small fruit grows into strong character.

PRAYER

God, Please grow good fruit in me. Help me choose love, peace, and self-control today. Change my heart from the inside. In Jesus' name, amen.

REMEMBER LINE

God grows good fruit in me as I obey Him.

WEEK 20: Peace-Maker

"Blessed are the peacemakers, for they will be called children of God." - Matthew 5:9

Two boys in Carter's class got into it during group work. Their voices got sharp. Chairs scraped. A few kids turned to watch, like it was a show.

Carter felt his heart beat faster. He didn't want to get pulled in. He also didn't want the fight to grow.

One boy said, "You always mess it up!" The other boy snapped back, "At least I'm doing something!"

Carter could have laughed along with the crowd. He could have whispered, "This is crazy," and stayed out of it.

Instead, he leaned in and said, "Hey. Let's slow down. We all want to finish."

Both boys looked at him.

Carter kept his voice steady. "What if we split the job? You do the writing, and you do the pictures. Then we can be done."

They didn't smile, but they stopped yelling. One of them shrugged. "Fine."

The room got quiet again. The teacher walked by and nodded.

After class, Carter felt shaky. He hadn't been loud or tough, but he had been brave.

<u>**WHAT IT MEANS**</u>

A peacemaker is not someone who avoids problems. A peacemaker steps in with wisdom to calm things down.

Peacemaking takes courage because you might be misunderstood. Some people think peace means being weak. But Jesus calls peacemakers "blessed." That means God smiles on this kind of strength.

Peacemaking also means you don't add fuel. You don't spread the drama. You don't jump into insults. You work toward what is right.

Sometimes peacemaking is simple:

✝ Use a calm voice.

✝ Suggest a fair plan.

✝ Admit your part.

✝ Say, "Let's fix this."

Sometimes, it also means getting an adult when things are getting unsafe. That is wise, not cowardly.

A brave heart makes peace when others want a fight.

<u>**STRONG STEP**</u>

Practice the **Peace Move** this week.

When you see conflict starting:

1. **Lower the heat:** speak softer, not louder.
2. **Say one calm sentence:** "Let's slow down." or "We can work this out."
3. **Offer one fair next step:** "Let's take turns," or "Let's split the job."

If the conflict feels unsafe, get help right away from a teacher, parent, or coach.

<u>**PRAYER**</u>

Jesus, Make me a peacemaker. Help me use calm words and wise actions. Give me courage to do what is right when others want to fight. In Your name, amen.

<u>**REMEMBER LINE**</u>

God calls me to make peace.

WEEK 21: Shine Where You Are

"In the same way, let your light shine before others, that they may see your good deeds and glorify your Father in heaven." - Matthew 5:16

Amir saw it happen near the lockers. A bigger kid knocked a smaller kid's books to the floor. Papers slid everywhere.

Some boys laughed. One boy pulled out his phone like he wanted to record it.

Amir felt that tight feeling in his stomach. He didn't want to get picked on too. He didn't want trouble.

Then he remembered a Bible phrase he'd heard: "Let your light shine."

Amir walked over and crouched down. "Hey, I've got you," he said to the smaller kid.

He started picking up papers and stacking books. Another boy paused, then joined in. The phone went back into the pocket.

The bigger kid rolled his eyes and walked away.

When the smaller kid stood up, he looked relieved. "Thanks," he said. "I didn't know what to do."

Amir shrugged, but inside he felt steady. He didn't throw punches. He didn't act tough. He just did what was right.

<u>**WHAT IT MEANS**</u>

Your "light" is the way you live when people are watching and when they are not. It's your kindness, your courage, your honesty, and your self-control.

Jesus says to let your light shine so others can see what is good and give glory to God. That means your actions can point people to God.

Shining doesn't mean showing off. It means you don't hide your faith. You choose good even when the crowd chooses mean.

You can shine in small ways:

- ✝ Help someone who is embarrassed.
- ✝ Include someone who is left out.
- ✝ Refuse to laugh at a cruel joke.
- ✝ Tell the truth when it costs you.

A brave heart shines because it belongs to Jesus.

<u>**STRONG STEP**</u>

Do **One Light Move** this week.

Pick one simple way to shine:

- ✝ Help someone carry something.
- ✝ Sit with a kid who is alone.
- ✝ Say "Stop" when someone is being teased.
- ✝ Send one kind message.
- ✝ Clean up a mess without being asked.

Do it quietly. Then thank God for giving you courage.

<u>**PRAYER**</u>

Jesus, Help my life shine in a way that honors You. Give me courage to do good when it's hard. Use me to help someone this week. In Your name, amen.

<u>**REMEMBER LINE**</u>

I can shine by doing what is right.

WEEK 22: God First

"But seek first his kingdom and his righteousness, and all these things will be given to you as well." - Matthew 6:33

STORY

Zach had been saving for a new game. He counted his money twice and felt proud. He was almost there.

Then his mom said, "We're collecting food at church this week. Do you want to give something?"

Zach's stomach tightened. If he gave money, it would take longer to buy the game.

That night, Zach saw a photo on the church board. It showed a family with a small pile of groceries on a table. The note said, "Thank you."

Zach thought about his pantry at home. He thought about how he had never wondered where his next meal would come from.

He opened his Bible and read: "Seek first the kingdom of God."

Zach prayed, "God, help me put You first." Then he took a few bills from his savings and placed them in an envelope.

On Sunday, he dropped it in the giving box. He still wanted the game. But he also felt something stronger than wanting. He felt joy, like he chose the better thing.

<u>**WHAT IT MEANS**</u>

To "seek first" means God comes before everything else. Not because God wants to take your fun, but because God wants your heart.

God first doesn't mean you never play games or enjoy sports. It means you don't let those things lead you. God leads you.

When you put God first, you ask questions like:

✝ "What would please God right now?"

✝ "Is this choice right?"

✝ "How can I love people today?"

"His righteousness" means choosing what is right in God's eyes. That includes how you spend your time, how you talk, and how you treat people.

A brave heart puts God first, even when it costs something.

<u>**STRONG STEP**</u>

Try the **First Place Check** this week.

Once each day, before you start your favorite thing (screen time, sports, hanging out), do one of these:

✝ Read one Bible verse.

✝ Pray for one minute.

✝ Do one helpful task at home.

✝ Choose one kind action for someone else.

Then say: **"God, You come first."**

It's small, but it trains your heart.

<u>**PRAYER**</u>

God, Help me seek You first. Show me what is right, and help me choose it. Teach me to love You more than my wants. In Jesus' name, amen.

<u>**REMEMBER LINE**</u>

God comes first in my choices.

WEEK 23: Win the Thought Fight

"We demolish arguments and every pretension that sets itself up against the knowledge of God, and we take captive every thought to make it obedient to Christ." - 2 Corinthians 10:5

Evan missed an easy goal in soccer. The ball rolled wide, and someone on the other team laughed.

Right away, a mean voice started talking in Evan's head: *You're terrible. Everyone saw. You always mess up.*

Evan's cheeks burned. He wanted to hide. He wanted to stop trying so he couldn't fail again.

At halftime, Evan sat on the bench and stared at his cleats. His coach walked by and said, "Shake it off. Keep your head up."

Evan nodded, but his thoughts were still loud.

Then Evan remembered part of a Bible phrase his grandma taught him: "We take captive every thought to make it obedient to Christ."

Evan whispered, "No." Not out loud. Just in his heart. He said, "That thought is not helping me."

He replaced it with truth: "I made a mistake, but I can keep going."

In the second half, Evan still felt nervous, but he ran. He passed. He tried again. And he played better because his mind wasn't beating him up anymore.

<u>**WHAT IT MEANS**</u>

Your thoughts can guide your life. A thought can push you toward sin, fear, or quitting. Or a thought can push you toward courage and truth.

This verse says you can "take" thoughts captive. That means you don't have to believe every thought that shows up in your mind.

Some thoughts are lies:

✝ "God doesn't care."

✝ "You'll never change."

✝ "You might as well do wrong."

✝ "You're worthless."

God's truth is different:

✝ God is with you.

✝ God forgives you when you confess.

✝ God can help you grow.

✝ Your life matters.

A brave heart fights the battle in the mind with God's truth.

<u>**STRONG STEP**</u>

Use the **Catch-Check-Change** plan this week.

1. **Catch** the thought: "What am I thinking right now?"
2. **Check** it: "Is it true? Is it kind? Does it match God's Word?"
3. **Change** it: replace it with a true sentence.

Examples:

✝ Lie: "I can't do this." Truth: "I can do the next step with God's help."

✝ Lie: "I have to get even." Truth: "I can choose peace."

Write one "truth sentence" on paper and read it every morning.

<u>**PRAYER**</u>

Jesus, Help me notice my thoughts. Show me what is false, and help me replace it with truth. Teach me to obey You with my mind. In Your name, amen.

<u>**REMEMBER LINE**</u>

I don't have to follow every thought.

WEEK 24: Enough Grace

"But he said to me, "My grace is sufficient for you, for my power is made perfect in weakness." Therefore I will boast all the more gladly about my weaknesses, so that Christ's power may rest on me." - 2 Corinthians 12:9

Seth had practiced his short speech all week. He could say it fine at home. But when he stood in front of the class, his throat went dry.

He started reading. Then he messed up a word. A couple kids snickered.

Seth's mind went blank. He rushed the rest, sat down fast, and stared at his desk. His ears felt hot.

All day he replayed it: *I sounded stupid. I ruined it.*

After school, Seth kicked at the sidewalk on the way home. His mom asked, "How was your day?"

Seth shrugged. Then the words came out. "I messed up in front of everyone."

His mom listened. "That hurts," she said. "But one moment doesn't decide who you are."

That night Seth read part of a Bible phrase: "My grace is sufficient for you."

Seth didn't feel happy about his speech, but he felt less crushed. God's grace was enough for his embarrassing moment too.

WHAT IT MEANS

Grace is God's help that you do not earn. It is also God's kindness when you fail.

Paul wrote this after he asked God to remove a hard thing from his life. God didn't remove it. God gave grace instead.

Sometimes, you want God to erase the problem. Sometimes God gives you strength to walk through it.

"My grace is sufficient" means this: God's grace is enough for today. Enough for your weakness. Enough for your mistakes. Enough for the thing you wish you could redo.

Grace doesn't mean sin is fine. It means you can repent and be forgiven. Grace doesn't mean you stop trying. It means you try again with God's help.

A brave heart doesn't quit after failure. It stands back up.

STRONG STEP

Practice the **Grace Talk** this week.

When you mess up, say three things:

1. **Admit it:** "I messed up."
2. **Ask God:** "Please forgive me and help me."
3. **Try again:** "What is my next right step?"

Then do one small repair:

- ✝ Apologize.
- ✝ Fix what you broke.
- ✝ Study and practice.
- ✝ Make a better choice next time.

PRAYER

God, Thank You for Your grace. When I feel weak or ashamed, help me remember You are still with me. Forgive me and help me grow. In Jesus' name, amen.

REMEMBER LINE

God's grace is enough for me today.

WEEK 25: Light in the Dark

Theo hated going into the garage at night. The light switch was on the far wall, and the space felt huge when it was dark.

One evening his dad asked, "Can you grab the toolbox from the garage?"

Theo tried to act normal. "Sure."

He opened the door a crack. The dark air smelled like oil and dust. His heart beat faster. His brain started making scary pictures, even though he knew it was just a garage.

Then Theo noticed the small flashlight on the shelf by the door. He picked it up and clicked it on. A bright beam cut through the dark.

Theo walked in slowly. The light showed what was really there: bikes, boxes, a ladder, and the toolbox. No mystery. No monsters. Just stuff.

He grabbed the toolbox and hurried back inside.

Later, Theo read this line in Psalm 27: "The LORD is my light." He smiled because he got it. God is like a light that shows what is true when fear tries to fool you.

<u>**WHAT IT MEANS**</u>

Darkness can make small things feel big. Fear can do the same in your mind. It can make you imagine the worst. It can make you feel trapped.

God says He is your light. Light helps you see. Light helps you walk. Light helps you move forward without guessing.

God is also your salvation. That means He saves. He rescues. He protects your soul. He is stronger than anything that scares you.

This verse doesn't mean you will never feel fear. It means you don't have to obey fear. When God is your light, you can take the next step.

A brave heart looks to God when fear shows up.

<u>**STRONG STEP**</u>

Try the **Flashlight Prayer** this week.

When you feel afraid:

1. Say: **"Lord, be my light."**
2. Name what is true: "God is with me."
3. Take one next step anyway.

You can also do something practical: turn on a light, talk to a trusted adult, or move to a safe place. Faith and wisdom work together.

<u>**PRAYER**</u>

Lord, Thank You for being my light. When I feel scared, help me remember what is true. Give me courage to take the next step. In Jesus' name, amen.

<u>**REMEMBER LINE**</u>

God is my light, so fear doesn't lead me.

WEEK 26: Joy Gives Strength

"Nehemiah said, "Go and enjoy choice food and sweet drinks, and send some to those who have nothing prepared. This day is holy to our Lord. Do not grieve, for the joy of the Lord is your strength." - Nehemiah 8:10

Parker had a rough week. He got in trouble for talking in class. He argued with his brother. Then he missed two easy shots at basketball practice.

By Friday, Parker felt done. He flopped on the couch and stared at the ceiling. "Everything's going wrong," he muttered.

His mom sat down beside him. "Want to help me with something?" she asked.

Parker didn't. But he followed her to the kitchen anyway.

She handed him a marker and a big paper. "Write down three good things from this week."

Parker frowned. "There aren't any."

His mom waited.

Parker finally wrote:

1. I got a good grade on my spelling test.
2. Coach said I hustle hard.
3. Grandma called me and prayed for me.

His mom smiled. "Now thank God for those."

Parker felt a small lift inside, like a window cracked open. The week was still hard, but hope was back.

That night Parker read part of a verse that said: "The joy of the LORD is your strength." He realized joy wasn't the same as pretending life is perfect. Joy was remembering God is good, even on rough days.

WHAT IT MEANS

Joy from God is deeper than a joke or a fun day. It is a steady gladness that comes from knowing God loves you and stays with you.

Nehemiah spoke these words when God's people were hearing God's Word again. They were emotional, but they also needed strength to keep going. God's joy would help them.

Joy doesn't mean you never feel sad. It means sadness doesn't get the final word. God is still faithful.

When you thank God and remember what is true, your heart gets stronger. You can stand back up. You can try again. You can forgive. You can keep going.

A brave heart learns to find God's joy.

STRONG STEP

Do the **3 Thanks** plan this week.

Each day, write or say three thank-yous to God:

- ✝ One small thing (a good meal, a friend, a sunny day).
- ✝ One hard thing God helped you handle.
- ✝ One promise from God (like "God is with me").

If your day feels bad, start small. Even "Thank You for breathing" counts.

PRAYER

God, Thank You for Your joy.

Please give me strength when my days feel hard. Help me remember what is good and true. In Jesus' name, amen.

REMEMBER LINE

God's joy makes me strong.

WEEK 27: Kind Is Strong

"Be kind and compassionate to one another, forgiving each other, just as in Christ God forgave you." - Ephesians 4:32

Hunter was walking to the bus when he saw a kid from his grade, Lucas, digging through his backpack. Papers were spilling out onto the sidewalk.

Two boys nearby snorted. One said, "Man, he's always a mess."

Lucas's hands shook as he tried to stuff everything back in. His face looked tired, like he wanted to disappear.

Hunter had a choice. He could keep walking and stay safe. Or he could help and risk getting noticed.

Hunter stepped over and crouched down. "Hey, I'll help," he said.

Lucas blinked. "Thanks."

Hunter picked up papers, folders, and a pencil case. He didn't make a big deal out of it. He just helped.

One of the boys watching said, "Why are you helping him?"

Hunter stood up and said, calm and simple, "Because it's kind."

The boys didn't have a great comeback. They just shrugged and looked away.

On the bus, Lucas whispered, "Thanks. I needed that."

Hunter sat back and thought, *That felt better than laughing.*

WHAT IT MEANS

Some people think kindness is soft. Like it means you're weak. But the Bible says kindness is part of a life that honors God.

Kindness takes courage. It can cost you something: attention, time, pride, or the chance to blend in.

Jesus was kind. He cared for people others ignored. He helped the hurting. He spoke truth without being cruel.

Kindness also protects your heart. Mean jokes and rude words can feel powerful for a moment, but they leave a mess inside. Kindness leaves peace.

A brave heart is strong enough to be kind, even when others are not.

STRONG STEP

Do a **Hidden Kindness** this week.

Pick one kind act and don't brag about it:

† Help someone pick up something they dropped.

† Hold the door and smile.

† Invite someone into your game.

† Send a short encouraging message.

† Sit with someone who's alone.

After you do it, say to God: **"Thank You for helping me be kind."**

PRAYER

God, Please make me a kind boy. Help me treat people the way You want me to. Give me courage to do good even when others laugh. In Jesus' name, amen.

REMEMBER LINE

Kindness is strong.

WEEK 28: Good Friends Make You Sharper

"As iron sharpens iron, so one person sharpens another."
- Proverbs 27:17

Miles and Jordan were on the same basketball team. They were also friends, but they weren't always easy on each other.

After practice, Jordan said, "You keep dropping passes."

Miles bristled. "So? You missed shots too."

Jordan shrugged. "Yeah. But if we want to win, we have to get better."

Miles wanted to stay mad. It felt nicer than admitting Jordan had a point.

Then Miles remembered something Coach always said: "Good teammates tell the truth."

The next practice, Miles asked Jordan, "Can you help me work on catching?"

Jordan nodded. "Sure. Ten minutes."

They stayed after and threw passes back and forth. Jordan didn't make fun of him. He pushed him, but in a helpful way. Miles started catching cleaner.

On the way home, Miles thought about the Bible phrase that mentions: "Iron sharpens iron." It didn't sound cozy. It sounded like work. But it also sounded like growth.

WHAT IT MEANS

Iron sharpening iron is a picture of friends helping each other grow stronger. Real friends don't just say what you want to hear. They help you become better.

That doesn't mean a friend is rude. A sharp friend is not a bully. A good friend tells the truth with respect and wants what is best for you.

Good friends can sharpen you in many ways:
- ✝ They help you make wise choices.
- ✝ They pull you away from trouble.
- ✝ They tell you when you're being selfish.
- ✝ They cheer you on when you're tired.
- ✝ They point you back to God.

A brave heart chooses friends who help, not friends who drag you down.

STRONG STEP

Do the **Friend Check** this week.

Think of your closest friends and ask:
- ✝ Do they help me obey God?
- ✝ Do I feel pushed toward good or toward trouble?
- ✝ Do we build each other up?

Then do one action:
- ✝ Thank a friend who sharpens you.
- ✝ Apologize if you've been a bad friend.
- ✝ Step back from a friendship that pulls you into sin.

If you're not sure, talk to a parent or trusted adult.

PRAYER

God, Thank You for friends. Help me choose friends who make me better, not worse. Help me be the kind of friend who sharpens others with love. In Jesus' name, amen.

REMEMBER LINE

Good friends help me grow stronger.

WEEK 29: Humble and Brave

Cole finally got his test back. Big red letters at the top said: **100%.**

Cole felt like he could float. At lunch he told his friends, "Easy. I didn't even study that much."

One friend said, "For real?" Cole smirked. "Yeah. I'm just good at this."

Across the table, a kid named Aaron stared at his tray. Aaron had been studying hard all week. Cole knew Aaron struggled in that class.

After lunch, Cole saw Aaron shove his paper into his backpack like he wanted it to disappear.

Cole's smile faded. He realized his words didn't just make him look good. They made Aaron feel small.

That night, Cole read: "God opposes the proud but shows favor to the humble."

Cole sat up in bed and whispered, "God, I acted proud. I'm sorry."

The next day Cole found Aaron and said, "Hey, I was bragging yesterday. That wasn't right. If you want, I can help you study next time."

Aaron looked surprised. Then he nodded. "Yeah. That would help."

WHAT IT MEANS

Pride says, "Look at me." Humility says, "God helped me, and I still have room to grow."

Humility is not pretending you're bad at everything. It's telling the truth without bragging. It's using your gifts to help others, not to step on them.

This verse is a warning and a promise:

✝ God opposes pride. Pride pushes God away.

✝ God gives grace to the humble. Humility pulls God close.

A humble boy can learn. A proud boy won't. A humble boy can say, "I was wrong." A proud boy makes excuses.

It takes bravery to be humble because pride feels safer. But humility is stronger. It keeps your heart teachable and your friendships healthy.

STRONG STEP

Try the **Humble Habit** this week.

When something goes well, do this:

1. **Give credit:** "Thank You, God."
2. **Stay kind:** don't brag or put others down.
3. **Lift someone up:** encourage or help someone who's struggling.

One sentence you can use:

✝ "I worked hard, and God helped me."

PRAYER

God, Please protect my heart from pride. Teach me to be humble and brave. Thank You for giving grace to the humble. Help me use my gifts to help others. In Jesus' name, amen.

REMEMBER LINE

Humility brings God's grace.

WEEK 30: Say No to Temptation

"Submit yourselves, then, to God. Resist the devil, and he will flee from you." - James 4:7

A group of boys crowded around Caleb's phone after school.

"Look at this," one boy said, grinning. "It's so funny."

Caleb leaned in. The clip started, and right away it felt wrong. It was mean. It made fun of someone who didn't deserve it.

A boy nudged Caleb. "Send it to the class chat."

Caleb felt pressure in his chest. If he said no, they might laugh at him. If he sent it, he would fit in.

Caleb's thumb hovered over the screen.

Then he remembered a Bible phrase: "Resist the devil."

Caleb locked the phone and stepped back. "Nah," he said. "I'm not sending that."

The boys groaned. One rolled his eyes. "Whatever."

Caleb's face got hot, but he stayed steady. He walked away.

Later, Caleb noticed something: the pressure didn't last forever. It faded the moment he chose the right thing.

<u>**WHAT IT MEANS**</u>

Temptation is a pull toward sin. Sometimes, it pulls you toward lies. Sometimes, it pulls you toward mean jokes. Sometimes, it pulls you toward stuff you shouldn't watch.

This verse says "resist." Resist means you push back. You don't play with temptation. You don't bargain with it. You say no and step away.

It also says the devil will flee. That means temptation can leave when you refuse it. It doesn't always leave in one second, but resisting is never wasted. Each time you resist, you get stronger.

God doesn't ask you to fight alone. The same verse says, "Submit yourselves therefore to God." When you submit to God, you choose His way first. Then you resist what is wrong.

A brave heart is not the boy who never feels tempted. A brave heart is the boy who says no.

<u>**STRONG STEP**</u>

Use the **Exit Plan** this week.

When temptation shows up:

1. **Say no out loud** if you can: "No. I'm not doing that."
2. **Move your body:** step back, walk away, close the screen.
3. **Replace it:** do something good right away (talk to a parent, read a verse, play outside, start homework).

If temptation keeps showing up online, ask a parent for help with controls. That is wise.

<u>**PRAYER**</u>

God, Help me submit to You today. Give me strength to resist what is wrong. Help me walk away fast and choose what is good. In Jesus' name, amen.

<u>**REMEMBER LINE**</u>

I can resist, and temptation can leave.

WEEK 31: God Sees Your Hurt

"The Lord is close to the brokenhearted and saves those who are crushed in spirit." - Psalm 34:18

Ben tried to act like he didn't care, but he did.

He had invited a few boys to come over on Saturday. One of them said, "Sure." Another said, "Maybe."

On Saturday morning, Ben checked his phone again. No replies. Then he saw pictures online. The boys were at another kid's house, laughing and eating pizza.

Ben's chest felt tight. He set his phone down and stared at the wall. He wanted to be angry. He also wanted to cry. Mostly he felt left out.

Ben walked outside and sat on the front step. He didn't know what to say to God. So he said the truth.

"God, that hurt."

He stayed quiet for a minute. The air was still. Then his little sister came out and sat beside him without talking.

Later that day, Ben opened his Bible and read: "The Lord is close to the brokenhearted."

Ben still didn't like what happened. But he felt less alone. God was close, even in the hurt.

WHAT IT MEANS

Some pain doesn't show on the outside. Feeling left out can hurt. Being laughed at can hurt. Losing someone can hurt. Family problems can hurt.

This verse is a promise: God comes near when your heart is broken. He doesn't tell you to "get over it." He doesn't shame you for feeling sad.

God is near. That means you can talk to Him honestly. You can tell Him what happened. You can ask for comfort and help.

Being brokenhearted doesn't mean you're weak. It means you're human. A brave heart doesn't hide pain behind a fake smile. A brave heart brings pain to God.

God can also use other people to comfort you, such as parents, friends, pastors, and trusted adults. Asking for help is a strong move.

STRONG STEP

Try the **Hurt to God** step this week.

When something hurts:

1. Say it to God in one sentence: "God, this hurt because   ."
2. Ask for help: "Please comfort me and guide me."
3. Take one wise action: talk to a parent, take a walk, write it down, or do something healthy.

If you keep feeling heavy for many days, tell an adult you trust. You don't have to carry it alone.

PRAYER

God, You see my heart. Thank You for being near when I hurt. Please comfort me and help me know what to do next. In Jesus' name, amen.

REMEMBER LINE

When my heart hurts, God is close.

WEEK 32: Hand God Your Worries

"Cast all your anxiety on him because he cares for you." -
1 Peter 5:7

Jasper had a big game on Saturday. His coach said scouts might be there. Jasper tried to act cool, but his thoughts wouldn't stop.

What if I mess up? What if I let the team down? What if I freeze?

On Thursday night, Jasper lay in bed staring at the ceiling. He kept replaying mistakes from the last game. His stomach felt tight.

Jasper grabbed his notebook from his desk. He wrote one sentence at the top: **"God cares for me."**

Then he made a short list of worries. He didn't write a paragraph. Just quick lines.

✝ "I'm scared I'll fail."

✝ "I'm scared people will laugh."

✝ "I'm scared I won't be good enough."

Jasper looked at the list and whispered, "God, I'm handing this to You."

He tore the page out, folded it, and set it inside his Bible.

He still cared about the game, but he felt calmer. His worries weren't sitting alone inside his chest anymore.

WHAT IT MEANS

This verse gives you two big truths.

First: you can "cast" your anxiety on God. Cast means throw it off, like taking off a heavy backpack and dropping it. You don't have to hold worry all day.

Second: God cares for you. Not just for "church people." For you. For your real life. For your heart and your choices.

Worry tells you, "You're on your own." God's Word tells you, "I care. Come to Me."

Casting doesn't mean you'll never feel anxious again. Worry may come back. When it does, you cast it again. Over and over, if needed.

A brave heart learns to hand worries to God instead of hiding them.

STRONG STEP

Do the **Cast It** habit this week.

1. Write one worry on a small paper.
2. Pray: "God, I give You this worry because You care for me."
3. Put the paper in your Bible or a jar labeled "God."

Each time the worry returns, touch the paper and pray again.

Then do one wise thing you can control: practice, study, apologize, or ask for help.

PRAYER

God, You care for me. I give You my worries right now. Please calm my heart and help me do the next right thing. In Jesus' name, amen.

REMEMBER LINE

God cares for me, so I can give Him my worries.

WEEK 33: Keep Going

"Let us not become weary in doing good, for at the proper time we will reap a harvest if we do not give up."
- Galatians 6:9

Troy was tired of being the "responsible one."

At home, he helped with dishes. At school, he tried to stay out of trouble. On his team, he tried to encourage others, but it felt like nobody noticed.

Then one day, Troy's little brother broke his headphones. Troy had saved for them for months. He wanted to explode.

His brother said, "I'm sorry," but Troy didn't answer. He walked to his room and shut the door.

He sat on his bed and stared at the broken headphones. A heavy thought came: *Why do I even try to do good? It never works out for me.*

Troy opened his Bible, not even sure why. His eyes landed on a line: "Let us not grow weary of doing good."

Troy took a slow breath. He didn't feel instantly happy, but he felt steady enough to do the right thing.

He walked back out and said, "I'm mad. But I forgive you. Next time, ask before you touch my stuff."

His brother nodded fast. "Okay."

Troy didn't feel weak. He felt strong, because he didn't quit doing good.

WHAT IT MEANS

Doing good can feel tiring. You might think, *Nobody cares.* You might think, *Other kids get away with stuff. Why can't I?*

God knows that feeling. That's why He tells you not to grow weary.

This verse is a reminder: doing good is worth it, even when you don't see results right away. God sees. God rewards in His time. And doing good shapes you into a strong man.

Sometimes the "good" is forgiving. Sometimes it's staying honest. Sometimes it's not joining in when others are mean. Sometimes it's doing your job at home without complaining.

A brave heart keeps going because God is watching and helping.

STRONG STEP

Try the **Good Again** plan this week.

When you feel like quitting:

1. Whisper: **"God, help me not get tired of doing good."**
2. Do one good thing anyway.
3. After, thank God for helping you.

Pick one "good thing" you can repeat all week:

† Speak kindly at home.

† Help one person at school.

† Finish work without cheating

† Pray before you react.

Small good choices add up.

PRAYER

God, Sometimes I get tired of doing what is right. Please give me strength to keep going. Help me do good even when nobody notices. In Jesus' name, amen.

REMEMBER LINE

I won't quit doing good.

WEEK 34: Run Your Race

"Therefore, since we are surrounded by such a great cloud of witnesses, let us throw off everything that hinders and the sin that so easily entangles. And let us run with perseverance the race marked out for us," -
Hebrews 12:1

Jude watched the awards at the end of the season. Some boys got trophies. Some boys got shout-outs. Jude clapped, but inside he felt a pinch.

He thought about his own season. He tried hard, but he wasn't the top player. He didn't get the biggest score. Nobody called his name.

On the way home, Jude said to his mom, "I guess I'm not that good."

His mom didn't argue. She asked, "Did you get better this season?"

Jude thought about it. He had learned to pass faster. He had practiced even when he didn't feel like it. He had stayed positive when others complained.

"Yeah," he said. "I did."

That night Jude read: "And let us run with perseverance the race marked out for us."

He realized something. God wasn't comparing him to the best kid on the team. God was calling him to run *his* race with endurance.

WHAT IT MEANS

Endurance means you keep going for a long time. It means you don't quit when it's slow or hard.

This verse calls life a race, but it's not a race against other people. It's a race of faith. It's about following Jesus over time.

Comparing can steal your joy. It can make you think you're worthless or make you act proud. Either way, it pulls your eyes off what God gave you to do.

God has set a race "before you." That means God has your own path for you—your gifts, your challenges, and your chances to do good.

A brave heart runs its own race and doesn't quit.

STRONG STEP

Try the **No-Compare Rule** this week.

When you catch yourself comparing, do this:

1. Say: **"That's not my race."**
2. Name one thing you can improve this week.
3. Practice it for **10 minutes** on three days.

Examples:

✝ One school skill (spelling, reading, math facts).
✝ One sport skill (dribbling, passing, footwork).
✝ One character skill (patience, kindness, self-control).

Endurance grows by small repeats.

PRAYER

Jesus, Help me run my race with endurance. Protect my heart from comparison. Help me keep growing, even when progress is slow. In Your name, amen.

REMEMBER LINE

I will run my race and keep going.

WEEK 35: Look to Jesus

"fixing our eyes on Jesus, the pioneer and perfecter of faith. For the joy set before him he endured the cross, scorning its shame, and sat down at the right hand of the throne of God." - Hebrews 12:2

Sam got distracted fast. That was just true about him.

During homework, he checked his phone. During chores, he wandered off. During practice, he watched what other kids were doing instead of listening.

One day at practice, Coach blew the whistle. "Sam, you're looking everywhere but where you need to look."

Sam's face got hot. He wanted to argue, but he knew it was true.

That night, Sam read a short line in the Bible: "Looking to Jesus."

Sam pictured it like this: if you're running and you keep turning your head, you trip. If you keep your eyes forward, you run straighter.

Sam prayed, "Jesus, help me look to You."

The next day, when he felt himself drifting, he whispered, "Eyes on Jesus." It didn't make him perfect, but it helped him refocus.

WHAT IT MEANS

To "look to Jesus" means you make Jesus your main focus. You learn from Him. You follow Him. You remember what He says is true.

When you look at others too much, you can get pulled into comparison, jealousy, or fear. When you look at your problems too much, you can feel crushed.

Looking to Jesus doesn't erase your problems. It helps you walk through them with steadiness. Jesus is the One who saves you. He is also the One who shows you how to live.

When you're tempted, look to Jesus. When you're worried, look to Jesus. When you feel left out, look to Jesus.

A brave heart keeps its eyes on Jesus, even when life is noisy.

STRONG STEP

Do the **Look Again** habit this week.

When you notice you're drifting, do this:

1. **Stop for one breath.**
2. Whisper: **"Jesus, help me."**
3. Do the next right thing.

Use it in three places:

✝ During schoolwork.

✝ During a hard talk.

✝ When you're online.

If you want, write "Look to Jesus" on a sticky note and put it where you'll see it.

PRAYER

Jesus, Help me keep my eyes on You. When I get distracted, bring me back. Teach me to follow You one step at a time. In Your name, amen.

REMEMBER LINE

I look to Jesus to stay steady.

WEEK 36: God's Word Works

"For the word of God is alive and active. Sharper than any double-edged sword, it penetrates even to dividing soul and spirit, joints and marrow; it judges the thoughts and attitudes of the heart." - Hebrews 4:12

Isaac kept a small Bible on his shelf, but most days it stayed closed.

One night he couldn't sleep. His mind kept replaying a mean comment he made earlier. He wished he could rewind time.

Isaac got out of bed and grabbed his Bible. He didn't know where to start, so he opened to a page with a bookmark his grandma had placed there.

His eyes landed on a verse about kindness. Isaac read it twice.

Nothing magical happened. The room didn't glow. But Isaac felt something shift. The verse didn't just sit on the page. It poked his heart. It showed him what was wrong. It also showed him what to do next.

The next day Isaac found the kid he had snapped at and said, "I was rude yesterday. I'm sorry."

Later Isaac thought, *God's Word did that. It moved me.*

<u>WHAT IT MEANS</u>

God's Word is not just an old book of sayings. The Bible says it is "living and active." That means it works in real life.

God uses His Word to:

- ✝ Show you what is true.
- ✝ Warn you when you're heading the wrong way.
- ✝ Comfort you when you're hurting.
- ✝ Guide you when you don't know what to do.

Sometimes, God's Word feels like a mirror. It shows you your heart. That can feel uncomfortable, but it is good. God corrects because He loves you.

A brave heart doesn't avoid God's Word. It listens, even when the Word challenges you.

STRONG STEP

Try the **One Verse Test** this week.

1. Read **one** Bible verse each day.
2. Ask: "What is this teaching me?"
3. Do **one** action from it.

Examples of actions:

- ✝ Apologize.
- ✝ Tell the truth.
- ✝ Help someone.
- ✝ Turn away from sin.
- ✝ Pray for someone.

Keep it small. God's Word works through small obedience.

PRAYER

God, Thank You for Your Word. Please make it come alive in my life. Help me obey what You show me. In Jesus' name, amen.

REMEMBER LINE

God's Word is alive, and it helps me change.

WEEK 37: Do What the Word Says

"Do not merely listen to the word, and so deceive yourselves. Do what it says." - James 1:22

Wes liked listening to Bible stories. He liked the parts where the heroes were brave.

But on Tuesday, real life showed up.

His mom asked him to clean his room before screen time. Wes said, "Okay," but he kept playing. Ten minutes turned into thirty.

His mom came back. "Wes, did you clean?"

Wes shrugged. "I was going to."

His mom didn't yell. She pointed at the mess. "You heard me. But you didn't do it."

That night at youth group, Wes heard a verse that felt like it was aimed right at him: "Be doers of the word, and not hearers only."

Wes thought, *I hear a lot. But do I obey?*

The next day, when his mom asked again, Wes stood up right away. He cleaned his room. It wasn't fun, but it felt good to follow through.

WHAT IT MEANS

Hearing God's Word is good. But God wants more than listening. He wants obedience.

A "hearer only" knows Bible facts but doesn't live them. That can trick you. You might think you're strong because you know verses. But strength is shown by what you do when nobody is clapping.

Doing the Word looks like this:

- ✝ Forgiving when you want revenge.
- ✝ Telling the truth when lying would be easier.
- ✝ Serving when you'd rather be lazy.
- ✝ Turning away from temptation right away.

Obedience is hard sometimes. But obedience makes your faith real. It also builds confidence because you know you can follow God in everyday moments.

A brave heart doesn't just learn God's Word. It lives it.

STRONG STEP

Try the **Right Away Rule** this week.

Pick one instruction you often delay:

- ✝ A chore.
- ✝ Homework.
- ✝ Getting ready.
- ✝ Turning off a screen.
- ✝ Apologizing.

When you hear it, do it **right away** without arguing.

Then tell God: **"Help me be a doer."**

PRAYER

God, Help me not just listen to Your Word. Help me obey You in real life. Give me strength to do the right thing right away. In Jesus' name, amen.

REMEMBER LINE

I will do what God says.

WEEK 38: Love People on Purpose

"The second is this: 'Love your neighbor as yourself.'
There is no commandment greater than these." -
Mark 12:31

Harper noticed the new kid on the bus. The kid sat alone, hood up, looking out the window.

Harper's friend whispered, "He's weird. Don't talk to him."

Harper didn't like that. But he also didn't want to be the next target.

When the bus hit a bump, the new kid's pencil case fell and spilled. Pencils rolled under seats.

A few kids laughed. The new kid scrambled to grab them fast.

Harper felt that nudge inside again: *Do something.*

So Harper slid out of his seat, reached down, and picked up pencils. He handed them back without making it a big deal.

The new kid said quietly, "Thanks."

Harper nodded. "No problem. I'm Harper."

The new kid's shoulders relaxed a little. "I'm Devon."

It wasn't a movie moment. Nobody clapped. But it was real love in a real place.

WHAT IT MEANS

Jesus said loving your neighbor is one of the greatest commands. A "neighbor" isn't only the person who lives next door. It's the person near you: the kid on your bus, the classmate in your group, the teammate who is struggling.

"To love as yourself" means you treat people the way you would want to be treated. If you dropped your stuff, you'd want help. If you were new, you'd want a friendly face. If you felt left out, you'd want someone to notice.

Love is not just a feeling. Love is a choice. It's on purpose.

A brave heart chooses love even when the crowd chooses mean.

STRONG STEP

Do one **Neighbor Move** this week.

Pick one action:

- ✝ Say hi to a new kid.
- ✝ Sit with someone who is alone.
- ✝ Help someone who dropped something.
- ✝ Invite someone into your game.
- ✝ Defend someone with calm words: "That's not cool."

Keep it simple. Do it with respect. Do it because God loves you.

PRAYER

God, Help me love people on purpose. Show me who needs kindness this week. Give me courage to do the loving thing. In Jesus' name, amen.

REMEMBER LINE

I choose love on purpose.

WEEK 39: Greatness Looks Like Service

"Not so with you. Instead, whoever wants to become great among you must be your servant," - Mark 10:43

At tryouts, everyone wanted to be captain.

Bennett did too. He wanted the title. He wanted people to listen to him. He wanted to feel important.

During drills, one kid kept messing up. His name was Rico. A few boys groaned every time Rico missed.

Bennett rolled his eyes. "Come on, man," he said, loud enough for others to hear.

Rico's shoulders dropped. He tried again, but he got worse.

After practice, Coach gathered the team. "Captains aren't just the best players," he said. "Captains help the team."

Bennett thought about Rico's face.

The next practice, Bennett walked over to Rico before drills. "Hey," he said, quieter this time. "I can show you the footwork if you want."

Rico looked surprised. "Yeah. That would help."

Bennett helped him for five minutes. Rico improved a little. More than that, he looked like he could breathe again.

Bennett felt something shift. Helping didn't make him smaller. It made him stronger.

WHAT IT MEANS

Jesus flipped the world's idea of greatness.

The world often says, "Great means being first." Jesus says, "Great means serving."

Serving means you use what you have to help others. It can be skill. It can be time. It can be patience. It can be encouragement.

This doesn't mean you let people boss you around. It means you choose to help instead of pushing people down.

When you serve, you start to lead like Jesus. And that takes real courage.

A brave heart doesn't chase attention. It chases love.

STRONG STEP

Try the **Serve to Lead** plan this week.

Pick one place you spend time: home, school, sports, or church. Then do one servant action there:

- ✝ Encourage someone who is struggling.
- ✝ Help clean up without being asked.
- ✝ Share credit instead of grabbing it.
- ✝ Teach someone a skill without making fun of them.

Do it quietly. Let your actions speak.

PRAYER

Jesus, Teach me what real greatness is. Help me serve others with a good attitude. Make me a leader who helps, not a leader who hurts. In Your name, amen.

REMEMBER LINE

Greatness looks like service.

WEEK 40: Heart Matters Most

"But the Lord said to Samuel, "Do not consider his appearance or his height, for I have rejected him. The Lord does not look at the things people look at. People look at the outward appearance, but the Lord looks at the heart."." - 1 Samuel 16:7

Kaden stood in front of the mirror before school. He fixed his hair. He checked his shirt. He wanted to look cool.

At lunch, he sat with his friends and tried to act like nothing bothered him. But inside, Kaden felt tense. He kept thinking about what people thought of him.

That afternoon, a younger kid dropped his lunch tray. Food splattered. The cafeteria went quiet for a second, then a few kids laughed.

Kaden's friends started laughing too. Kaden smiled a little, like he was supposed to.

Then he saw the younger kid's face. It was red. His eyes looked watery.

Kaden felt a tug in his chest. He could keep laughing to fit in. Or he could do the right thing.

Kaden stood up, grabbed napkins, and walked over. "Hey," he said, "it's okay. I'll help."

His friends stopped laughing. One of them said, "Why are you doing that?"

Kaden didn't know how to explain it. He just said, "Because he needs help."

That night, Kaden read: "The Lord looks on the heart." He thought, *God cares more about who I am inside than how I look outside.*

WHAT IT MEANS

People can only see the outside. They see clothes, hair, and the way you act in public.

But God sees deeper. God sees your thoughts, your motives, and your choices when nobody is cheering.

In the story of 1 Samuel, people thought the biggest and strongest man would be chosen. But God chose David, a young shepherd. Why? Because God saw David's heart.

This is good news. If you feel overlooked, God still sees you. It's also a challenge. If you look good on the outside but act mean on the inside, God sees that too.

A brave heart cares about the heart. It chooses kindness, truth, and humility even when nobody is watching.

STRONG STEP

Do the **Heart Check** once each day this week.

Ask yourself:

1. "What is my heart aiming at today?"
2. "Am I trying to please people or please God?"
3. "What is one kind thing I can do?"

Then do one small heart choice: help, forgive, tell the truth, or include someone.

PRAYER

God, Thank You that You see my heart. Please clean my heart and guide my choices. Help me care more about what You think than what others think. In Jesus' name, amen.

REMEMBER LINE

God sees my heart, so I choose what is right.

WEEK 41: Choose God Today

"But if serving the Lord seems undesirable to you, then choose for yourselves this day whom you will serve, whether the gods your ancestors served beyond the Euphrates, or the gods of the Amorites, in whose land you are living. But as for me and my household, we will serve the Lord." - Joshua 24:15

Leo's friends had a new joke. It wasn't a clean joke. It was the kind of joke that made someone else look stupid.

At first, Leo didn't laugh. But then his friend stared at him and said, "Bro, don't be so serious."

Leo felt that tight pressure in his chest. He didn't want to be "the weird one." He didn't want to lose his place in the group.

His mind started making deals. *I'll just laugh a little. I won't say anything. It's not that bad.*

Then Leo remembered a Bible line he had heard before: "Choose this day."

That verse didn't feel old. It felt like right now.

Leo took a breath and said, calm and short, "I'm not into that."

One boy rolled his eyes. Another shrugged. Then the group moved on to something else.

Leo's heart still beat fast, but he felt clean inside. He chose God in a small moment, and it mattered.

WHAT IT MEANS

Joshua spoke these words to God's people. He told them they had to choose who they would serve.

You have choices too. Not once in your life, but every day.

You choose with your words. You choose with what you watch. You choose with what you laugh at. You choose with who you follow.

Serving God doesn't mean you are perfect. It means God is your leader. When you mess up, you confess and come back.

Choosing God is brave because it can cost you approval. But it also brings peace. Sin makes your heart feel heavy. Obedience makes your heart feel steady.

A brave heart chooses God today, not "someday."

STRONG STEP

Do the **Daily Choice** this week.

Each morning, say one sentence: **"God, today I choose to serve You."**

Then pick one area to watch closely:

- ✝ Words.
- ✝ Screens.
- ✝ Friends.
- ✝ Attitude.
- ✝ Honesty.

When pressure shows up, repeat: **"I choose God."**

PRAYER

God, Help me choose You today. Give me courage when others push me toward wrong. Help me serve You with my words and choices. In Jesus' name, amen.

REMEMBER LINE

Today, I choose God.

WEEK 42: Strong Joy

"A cheerful heart is good medicine, but a crushed spirit dries up the bones." - Proverbs 17:22

Jace woke up in a bad mood. Nothing big had even happened. He just felt grumpy.

At breakfast, he complained about the cereal. At school, he rolled his eyes at the teacher. At recess, he snapped at his friend for a small mistake.

By lunchtime, Jace felt worse, not better.

On the way home, his grandma called. "How's my guy?"

Jace almost said, "Fine," and ended it. But Grandma always seemed to know.

He sighed. "I've been in a bad mood all day."

Grandma didn't laugh at him. She said, "Let's try something. Find one good thing and thank God for it."

Jace looked out the window. The sky was bright blue. He said, "Okay ... the weather is nice."

Grandma said, "Good. Now find one more."

Jace thought. "My friend still played with me, even after I was rude."

Grandma said, "That's a gift."

When Jace hung up, he didn't feel like a superhero. But his mood loosened. His heart felt lighter.

That night, he read: "A cheerful heart is good medicine." He realized cheer isn't fake. It's a choice to notice good and give thanks.

WHAT IT MEANS

A cheerful heart doesn't mean you laugh all the time. It means your heart isn't stuck in grumbling.

Grumbling can spread like a cold. It can make your whole day feel sick. But a cheerful heart can help you heal inside. That's why the Bible calls it "good medicine."

This verse doesn't tell you to ignore pain. If you're hurting, tell God the truth. But even in hard times, you can still look for God's gifts: a friend, a meal, a safe place, a new chance.

Cheer also helps other people. One thankful boy can lift a whole room.

A brave heart chooses gratitude instead of grumbling.

STRONG STEP

Try the **Medicine List** this week.

Once each day, name **two** good things:

1. One good thing God gave you today.
2. One good thing you can do for someone else today.

Examples:

† "Thank You for lunch." / "I will encourage my friend."

† "Thank You for my bed." / "I will help my mom."

If you snapped at someone, add this: apologize fast.

PRAYER

God, Thank You for the good gifts You give me. Help me have a cheerful heart. Forgive me when I complain and snap at people. Teach me to be thankful. In Jesus' name, amen.

REMEMBER LINE

Gratitude makes my heart stronger.

WEEK 43: God Fights for You

"The Lord will fight for you; you need only to be still." -
Exodus 14:14

Mason's class had to do group presentations. Mason didn't mind speaking, but he hated unfair blame.

During prep, one boy in Mason's group didn't do his part. He joked around instead. Then, right before the presentation, he said, "We're not ready because Mason didn't finish the slides."

Mason's face got hot. That wasn't true.

Mason wanted to clap back. He wanted to embarrass the boy in front of everyone.

But Mason paused. He remembered a Bible line his dad had read at breakfast: "The Lord will fight for you."

Mason took a breath and chose steady words. He raised his hand and said, "I finished my part. We're missing one section. We can still present, and we'll turn in the missing part after class."

The teacher nodded. "Okay. Present what you have."

After class, the teacher asked a few questions and saw what happened. Mason didn't have to scream or insult anyone. The truth came out.

On the walk home, Mason felt calm. God had helped him stay steady.

WHAT IT MEANS

In Exodus, God's people were trapped with the sea in front and an army behind. They felt helpless. God told them, "The Lord will fight for you."

That doesn't mean you never speak up. It means you don't have to fight with sin. You don't have to use lies, rage, or payback to defend yourself.

Sometimes God fights for you by bringing truth to light. Sometimes He gives you wisdom to respond the right way. Sometimes He uses an adult to step in. Sometimes He gives you peace while you wait.

Your job is to do what is right and trust God with the result.

A brave heart can stay calm because God is bigger than the problem.

STRONG STEP

Try the **Calm Defense** this week.

When someone blames you or tries to start drama:

1. **Pause and pray:** "God, fight for me."
2. **Speak truth:** short, clear, no insults.
3. **Get help if needed:** teacher, parent, coach.

A good sentence to use:

✝ "That's not true. Here's what happened."

Then let God handle the rest.

PRAYER

God, Thank You that You fight for me. Help me stay calm and speak truth. Protect me from anger and payback. In Jesus' name, amen.

REMEMBER LINE

I can stay calm because God fights for me.

WEEK 44: God Will Not Leave You

"Be strong and courageous. Do not be afraid or terrified because of them, for the Lord your God goes with you; he will never leave you nor forsake you." - Deuteronomy 31:6

A new kid moved into Jonah's neighborhood. His name was Temba. He had a different accent and a different school uniform.

On the first day, Temba walked to the bus stop alone. A few kids stared. One boy whispered, "He talks funny."

Jonah felt nervous. He didn't want to get pulled into mean stuff. He also didn't want Temba to feel alone.

Jonah stepped closer and said, "Hey. I'm Jonah. Want to stand here with me?"

Temba looked surprised. "Okay," he said.

They waited together. The bus felt loud, but standing next to someone helped. Jonah asked, "What games do you like?" Temba smiled and said, "Soccer."

After school, Jonah thought about how scary new places can feel. He opened his Bible and read: "He will not leave you or forsake you."

Jonah realized God's promise wasn't only for the new kid. It was for him too. God stays.

WHAT IT MEANS

"Leave" means walk away. "Forsake" means abandon. God says He will do neither.

People sometimes leave. Friends move. Plans change. Feelings shift. But God stays faithful.

This promise is for scary moments, like starting a new school, joining a new team, or walking into a hard conversation. God's presence doesn't depend on your mood. He is with you because He is God.

This also helps you treat others well. When you know God won't abandon you, you can be brave enough to stand beside someone who feels alone.

A brave heart stands steady because God stays close.

STRONG STEP

Do the **Not-Left Plan** this week.

1. Each morning say: **"God, You will not leave me."**
2. Look for one person who seems alone.
3. Do one simple action: say hi, invite them, or stand with them.

If you feel lonely, tell God and tell a trusted adult. You're not meant to carry loneliness by yourself.

PRAYER

God, Thank You that You will not leave me. Help me remember You are close when I feel alone. Use me to help someone else feel less alone too. In Jesus' name, amen.

REMEMBER LINE

God stays with me.

WEEK 45: Be Still

"He says, "Be still, and know that I am God; I will be exalted among the nations, I will be exalted in the earth." - Psalm 46:10

Noah's phone kept buzzing. Messages. Clips. Notifications. It felt like his brain never got a break.

One night, Noah climbed into bed and tried to sleep, but his mind was loud. He kept thinking about a comment someone left on his post. He kept wondering what people thought of him.

Noah sat up and turned his phone face-down on his desk.

He didn't know what to do next, so he did something simple. He sat on the edge of his bed and stayed quiet.

At first it felt weird. Then it felt peaceful.

Noah opened his Bible and read: "Be still, and know that I am God."

He took a slow breath and whispered, "God, You're in charge. I'm not."

After a few minutes, Noah felt calmer. The problems didn't vanish, but his heart settled down.

WHAT IT MEANS

Being still doesn't mean doing nothing all day. It means you stop the noise long enough to remember who God is.

When life is loud, it's easy to forget: God is in control. God is wise. God is strong. God is near.

Stillness helps you hear what matters. It helps your heart stop racing. It helps you pray without rushing.

A brave heart can be still. It doesn't need nonstop noise to feel okay.

STRONG STEP

Try the **Two-Minute Still** this week.

Once each day:

1. Put your phone away.
2. Sit still for **two minutes.**
3. Breathe slowly and pray one sentence: **"God, You are God. Please guide me."**

If your mind wanders, don't quit. Just come back to the sentence.

PRAYER

God, Help me be still and remember You are God. Calm my thoughts and lead my choices. Thank You for being in control. In Jesus' name, amen.

REMEMBER LINE

Stillness helps me remember God is in charge.

WEEK 46: Clean Again

"If we confess our sins, he is faithful and just to forgive us our sins and to cleanse us from all unrighteousness." -
1 John 1:9

Ryan got mad during a game at recess. A boy bumped him, and Ryan shoved back hard.

The boy fell. Kids gasped. A teacher blew the whistle and called Ryan over.

Ryan's stomach dropped. He wanted to blame the other boy. He wanted to say, "He started it." But he knew his shove was wrong.

All day Ryan felt heavy. He kept thinking, *I messed up. I'm in trouble. God must be disappointed.*

After dinner, Ryan sat in his room and stared at the floor. He didn't want to pray. He felt too dirty inside.

Then he remembered a Bible verse his mom had taught him: "If we confess our sins ..."

Ryan whispered, "God, I sinned. I shoved him. I was wrong."

He waited, expecting to feel worse. But he felt relief instead, like he finally took off a muddy coat.

The next day Ryan found the boy and said, "I'm sorry I shoved you. That was wrong." The boy nodded. "It's okay."

Ryan still had to face consequences at school, but his heart felt clean again.

WHAT IT MEANS

To confess means you tell the truth about your sin. You don't hide it. You don't excuse it. You don't blame others.

This verse gives you a strong promise: God is faithful and just to forgive. That means God keeps His word. When you confess, He forgives because Jesus paid for sin.

God also "cleanses" you. That means He washes your heart. Shame says, "You're stuck." God says, "Come back."

Confession doesn't remove consequences. You may still need to fix what you broke. But confession brings you back to God. It brings peace.

A brave heart admits sin and comes to God quickly.

STRONG STEP

Use the **Clean Again Steps** this week if you mess up:

1. **Confess to God:** "I sinned by ."
2. **Ask forgiveness:** "Please forgive me."
3. **Make it right:** apologize, replace, repair, or tell the truth.

If you keep struggling with the same sin, tell a trusted adult. That is wisdom, not shame.

PRAYER

God, Thank You that You forgive me when I confess. Please cleanse my heart and help me change. Help me make things right when I do wrong. In Jesus' name, amen.

REMEMBER LINE

When I confess, God cleans my heart.

WEEK 47: Fear Has to Go

"There is no fear in love. But perfect love drives out fear, because fear has to do with punishment. The one who fears is not made perfect in love." - 1 John 4:18

Eli heard thunder before he saw lightning. The sky went dark, and the wind pushed rain against the window.

Eli didn't like storms. He tried to act normal, but his stomach felt jumpy. He kept checking the sky like he could control it by watching.

Then the power flickered. The lights blinked off. The house went quiet except for rain and distant thunder.

Eli's heart raced. He grabbed his blanket and walked quickly to the living room where his mom was lighting a candle.

His mom looked up. "Storms can feel scary," she said. "Want to sit with me?"

Eli sat down and held his blanket tight.

His mom opened her Bible and read one short line: "Perfect love casts out fear."

Eli asked, "What does that mean?"

His mom answered right away. "It means God's love is stronger than fear. Fear tries to boss you. God's love pushes fear out."

Eli listened to the thunder again. He still didn't like it. But he felt safer. He prayed, "God, thank You for loving me. Help me not be afraid."

WHAT IT MEANS

Fear is real. It can show up in storms, in the dark, in a new place, or in a hard day at school.

This verse doesn't say, "Fear is silly." It says God's love is stronger.

God's love is "perfect" because it doesn't quit. It doesn't depend on your mood. It doesn't disappear when you mess up. God proved His love by sending Jesus to save you.

When you remember God's love, fear loses power. You can still feel scared, but you don't have to obey fear. You can pray. You can breathe. You can take the next step.

A brave heart leans on God's love.

STRONG STEP

Try the **Love Over Fear** plan this week.

When fear shows up:

1. Say: **"God loves me."**
2. Pray: "God, help me be brave."
3. Do one calming action: breathe slowly, turn on a light, or sit near a trusted adult.

If fear keeps coming back often, tell a parent or caregiver. Getting help is strong.

PRAYER

God, Thank You for loving me. When I feel afraid, help me remember Your love is stronger. Give me peace and courage. In Jesus' name, amen.

REMEMBER LINE

God's love is stronger than my fear.

WEEK 48: Safe Place

"God is our refuge and strength, an ever-present help in trouble." - Psalm 46:1

Ari got a knot in his stomach when he saw the note on his desk: **"Meet me after school."** No name.

All day he wondered who wrote it and why. His mind made a hundred guesses. By the last period, Ari's hands felt sweaty.

After school he walked outside slowly. He looked around, trying to spot trouble.

It turned out the note was from his teacher. She wanted to talk about a missing assignment and help him make a plan. Ari felt silly, but also relieved.

On the walk home, Ari thought, *I spent all day scared, and it wasn't even what I imagined.*

That night, Ari read: "God is our refuge and strength."

He pictured a refuge like a strong shelter in a storm. A place you can run to when life feels loud or scary.

Ari whispered, "God, You're my safe place."

<u>**WHAT IT MEANS**</u>

A refuge is a safe shelter. Strength is steady power.

This verse means you don't have to face fear alone. God is not far away. He is a place you can run to in prayer. He is strength when you feel weak.

Being a Christian doesn't mean nothing scary happens. It means you have a safe place in God when scary things do happen.

God can calm your heart. He can guide your steps. He can give you wisdom to talk to a trusted adult when you need help.

A brave heart runs to God first.

<u>**STRONG STEP**</u>

Use the **Refuge Routine** this week when you feel stressed.

1. Stop and breathe once.
2. Pray: **"God, be my refuge and strength."**
3. Do one wise next step: ask a question, tell a parent, or start the task you're worried about.

You can also make a "refuge spot" at home—a chair or corner where you can pray for two minutes.

<u>**PRAYER**</u>

God, Thank You for being my refuge and strength. When I feel scared or stressed, help me run to You. Give me wisdom and peace. In Jesus' name, amen.

<u>**REMEMBER LINE**</u>

God is my safe place.

WEEK 49: Praise Out Loud

"Let everything that has breath praise the LORD." -
Psalm 150:6

Ethan had a day he didn't like. He forgot his lunch. He got called on in class and didn't know the answer. Then a friend ignored him at recess.

By the time he got home, Ethan felt sour inside. He tossed his backpack down and flopped on his bed.

His dad knocked and stepped in. "How was your day?"

Ethan shrugged. "Bad."

His dad nodded. "Want to try something that helps me?"

Ethan didn't really want to. But he said, "Okay."

His dad said, "Stand up. Take one breath. Then thank God out loud for one thing."

Ethan felt silly, but he tried. He took a breath and said, "Thank You, God ... that I'm home."

His dad smiled. "Good. One more."

Ethan looked around. "Thank You... for my bed."

His dad said, "Last one."

Ethan thought harder. "Thank You for Mom making dinner."

After that, Ethan didn't suddenly love his day. But he felt lighter. The sour feeling didn't rule him anymore.

That night, Ethan read: "Let everything that has breath praise the LORD!" He realized praise wasn't only for great days. It was also for hard days.

WHAT IT MEANS

Praise means you tell God the truth about who He is. You thank Him. You honor Him.

This verse says "everything that has breath." That includes you. If you can breathe, you can praise.

Praise doesn't mean you pretend life is perfect. It means you remember God is still good. It lifts your eyes from only your problems and helps your heart stand up again.

Praise can also guard you. It keeps anger from growing. It keeps sadness from taking over. It reminds you that God is bigger than one rough day.

A brave heart can praise God out loud, even when it feels awkward.

STRONG STEP

Try the **Breath Praise** plan this week.

Once each day, do this:

1. Take one slow breath.
2. Say out loud: **"God, You are good."**
3. Thank Him for **three** things.

Keep them simple:

✝ "Thank You for food."

✝ "Thank You for a safe place."

✝ "Thank You for one friend."

✝ "Thank You for helping me today."

If you don't feel thankful, start with breath: "Thank You that I can breathe."

PRAYER

God, Thank You for giving me breath. Help me praise You, even on hard days. Fill my heart with hope and peace. In Jesus' name, amen.

REMEMBER LINE

As long as I can breathe, I can praise God.

WEEK 50: Thanks in Every Season

"give thanks in all circumstances; for this is God's will for you in Christ Jesus." - 1 Thessalonians 5:18

Omar's week had two kinds of days.

On Monday, he got picked for a group he wanted. On Tuesday, he lost his temper and got in trouble. On Wednesday, his team won. On Thursday, he bombed a quiz.

Omar felt like his mood kept swinging. Good day: happy. Bad day: grumpy.

On Friday night, Omar's mom handed him a small jar and some paper slips. She wrote on the jar: **"Thanks."**

"What's that for?" Omar asked.

His mom said, "For every season. Good ones and hard ones."

Omar shrugged. "How do you give thanks on bad days?"

His mom answered right away. "You thank God for what is still true, even when your day isn't great."

Omar tried it. He wrote:

- ✝ "Thank You for my family."
- ✝ "Thank You that I can try again."
- ✝ "Thank You that You forgive me when I confess."

He dropped the slips into the jar. His problems didn't disappear. But he felt steadier.

Later, Omar read: "Give thanks in all circumstances." It sounded like God wanted him to be strong and thankful in every season, not only the easy ones.

WHAT IT MEANS

"All circumstances" means every kind of day. Great days and rough days.

This verse doesn't say, "Give thanks *for* everything." Some things are sad and wrong. But you can still give thanks *in* every situation because God is still with you.

When life is good, gratitude keeps you humble. When life is hard, gratitude keeps you hopeful.

Giving thanks is also a choice. Your feelings might say, "Complain." God's Word says, "Give thanks." A brave heart chooses God's way.

STRONG STEP

Do the **Thanks Jar** this week.

1. Find a jar, cup, or envelope.
2. Each day, write **one** thank-you to God and put it inside.
3. On the weekend, read the slips out loud.

If your day is rough, use one of these starters:

- ✝ "Thank You that You are with me."
- ✝ "Thank You that I can start again."
- ✝ "Thank You for one good thing today."

PRAYER

God, Help me give thanks in every kind of day. Open my eyes to Your gifts. Keep my heart steady in good times and hard times. In Jesus' name, amen.

REMEMBER LINE

I can thank God in every season.

WEEK 51: God Sings Over You

"The Lord your God is with you, the Mighty Warrior who saves. He will take great delight in you; in his love he will no longer rebuke you, but will rejoice over you with singing." - Zephaniah 3:17

Calvin messed up at school and got called to the office. He didn't do something huge, but it was enough to feel embarrassed.

On the way home, Calvin kept thinking, *Everyone thinks I'm the bad kid.* He felt a heavy shame in his chest.

At home, Calvin went straight to his room. He didn't want dinner. He didn't want jokes. He just wanted to disappear.

His aunt knocked softly. "Can I come in?"

Calvin didn't answer, but she came in anyway and sat on the floor by the door.

After a quiet minute she said, "I'm not here to yell. I'm here because I love you."

Calvin's eyes stung. "I messed up."

His aunt nodded. "Yes. And you can make it right. But listen—God doesn't stop loving you when you fail."

She opened her Bible and read: "He will rejoice over you with singing."

Calvin blinked. "God sings?"

His aunt smiled. "That's what the verse says. God takes joy in His people. He's not waiting to crush you. He wants to bring you close."

Calvin still had to face consequences. But shame didn't feel like a cage anymore. God's love felt bigger.

WHAT IT MEANS

This verse is a picture of God's heart. God isn't cold. He isn't mean. He isn't far away.

God "rejoices" over His people. That means He feels joy. And the verse says "with singing." It's like God's love is so full it overflows.

This does not mean sin is no big deal. Sin matters. But God invites you to confess, repent, and return. He is ready to forgive because of Jesus.

If you belong to Jesus, you are not trash. You are not a mistake. You are loved.

A brave heart stands up again because it knows God's love is real.

STRONG STEP

Try the **Loved Truth** step this week.

When shame shows up, do this:

1. Say: **"God loves me."**
2. Confess what you did wrong if you need to.
3. Take one repair step: apologize, tell the truth, or fix what you broke.

Then read Zephaniah 3:17 again. Let God's love be louder than your shame.

PRAYER

God, Thank You that You love me. When I feel ashamed, help me run to You, not away. Help me confess, make things right, and start again. In Jesus' name, amen.

REMEMBER LINE

God loves me, even when I mess up.

WEEK 52: Finish Faithful

"His master replied, 'Well done, good and faithful servant! You have been faithful with a few things; I will put you in charge of many things. Come and share your master's happiness!'" - Matthew 25:21

It was the last week of the school year, and Tyler was tired.

He had started the year strong. But now he wanted to coast. He wanted to slack on chores, rush homework, and do the bare minimum.

On Wednesday, Tyler's coach ran a final hard practice. Tyler groaned. "Why are we doing this? The season is basically over."

Coach heard him. He didn't yell. He said, "Because finish matters."

That night, Tyler thought about that sentence: finish matters.

He opened his Bible and read: "Well done, good and faithful servant."

Tyler pictured standing before Jesus one day. He didn't picture Jesus asking, "Were you the best?" He pictured Jesus asking, "Were you faithful?"

The next day, Tyler chose one thing to finish well. He cleaned up after dinner without being asked. Then he finished a homework assignment he had been putting off.

It wasn't a huge moment. But it felt strong.

<u>**WHAT IT MEANS**</u>

In Jesus' story, a master praised a servant for being faithful. Faithful means you can be trusted. It means you keep doing what is right, even when it's boring, even when nobody is watching.

God doesn't only care about how you start. He cares about how you finish.

Finishing faithful can look like:

- ✝ Obeying God when you're tired.
- ✝ Telling the truth even at the end.
- ✝ Keeping your promises.
- ✝ Staying kind even when others are annoyed.
- ✝ Doing your work with honesty.

This isn't about earning God's love. God loves you because of Jesus. This is about living a life that pleases Him.

A brave heart finishes well.

<u>**STRONG STEP**</u>

Do the **Finish One Thing** plan this week.

Pick one thing you've been avoiding and finish it:

- ✝ A chore you keep delaying.
- ✝ A school task.
- ✝ An apology you need to make.
- ✝ Cleaning your room.
- ✝ Returning something you borrowed.

Do it fully. Then tell God: **"I want to be faithful."**

If you want a bonus, look back over your year and thank God for one way you grew.

<u>**PRAYER**</u>

Jesus, Help me be faithful. Help me finish what I start and do what is right. Thank You for walking with me all year. In Your name, amen.

<u>**REMEMBER LINE**</u>

I will finish faithful.

Welcome Aboard, Check Out This Limited-Time Free Bonus!

Ahoy, reader! Welcome to the Ahoy Publications family, and thanks for snagging a copy of this book! Since you've chosen to join us on this journey, we'd like to offer you something special.

Check out the link below for a FREE e-book filled with delightful facts about American History.

But that's not all - you'll also have access to our exclusive email list with even more free e-books and insider knowledge. Well, what are ye waiting for? Click the link below to join and set sail toward exciting adventures in American History.

Access your bonus here

https://ahoypublications.com/

Or, Scan the QR code!

www.ingramcontent.com/pod-product-compliance
Lightning Source LLC
Chambersburg PA
CBHW071446130726
47997CB00006B/2252